THE CAMEL, THE LION AND THE CHILD

A Cold War biography
based on Friedrich Nietzsche's fable
of self-realisation – his story of the self.

by MARTIN KNOX

First Published – 2024
This edition published 2024 by Novel Ideas
Brisbane, Qld
Australia

Copyright © Martin Knox 2024

 A catalogue record for this work is available from the National Library of Australia

The National Library of Australia Cataloguing-in-Publication

Creator: Knox, Martin, author.

Title: The Camel, The Lion and The Child.

ISBN: 978-0-6489930-8-7

Subjects: Biography

All rights reserved
No part of this book may be reproduced in any form, by photocopying or by any electronic or mechanical means, including information storage or retrieval systems, without prior permission in writing from both the copyright owner and the publisher of this book.
The author asserts his moral rights.
The Camel the Lion and the Child is a memoir of real events in the careers of Self, loosely associated with the author's experiences, which he relates to a fantasy story of the same title, written by Friedrich Nietzsche, first published in 1883. Martin Knox has changed names of characters, embellished incidents, added a few fictional characters and created dialogues in order to preserve authenticities of sequence and events while protecting individuals. Timings and content of Cold War events are indicative only.
Any resemblance to actual persons living or dead, businesses, companies, events, or locales is coincidental, for purposes of allegory or satire.

Typeset in Times New Roman 12pt by Donna Munro Graphic Design.
Cover artwork by Donna Munro Graphic Design.
Printed and bound in Australia by Ingram Spark.
Copyright © Martin Knox 2024
Publisher: Novel Ideas, West End, Brisbane.
htttps://www.martinknox.com
martinknx46@gmail.com

DEDICATION

In this book I have wanted to follow Nietzsche and excise religion, morality, history and tradition from the body of my life's work, embalming the remainder with the transcendent spirit that the philosopher used to imbue his heroes with creativity, daring, courage and self-mastery. It is dedicated to my family: Zoe, Tessa, Amani, Uly and Dorian, hoping that my writing will help them to respect, understand and conserve the World they will inherit, with care for living things, especially humans, animals and environments, through philosophies of freedom, voluntary responsibility, reason and science. Above all that they will abjure war and violence. I appreciate their support but opinions and any errors are my own.

Acknowledgements

I am indebted to the following.

Donna Munro has looked after the formatting, cover design and publishing.

The University of the Third Age's philosophy discussion group Matter's Arising, led by Garth Sherman, was a forum where group members' ideas were shared and opinions aired.

Dave Jones, discussed some of the ideas and philosophies with me, between songs with our guitars. He recommended the revolutionary politics of Che Guevara, in the posthumous movie of his memoirs, The Motorcycle Diaries, 2004.

Sam Adams of the University of Queensland's student philosophy association led discussion of the writings of Darwin, Nietzsche, Marx, Russell, Kaczynski, Foucault and Debord. The discussions helped interpret Nietzsche's allegory in relation to other philosophies.

Sunnybank Hills Writers Group, Maureen, Mark and Eve read our drafts carefully and together critically developed and explored writing ideas.

Brisbane Classic Books Meet Up discussed several classic fiction novels with ideas for this one.

AUTHOR BIO

Martin Knox grew up on a farm in Somerset England. He rode a horse and played rugby. He graduated as a chemical engineer from Birmingham University and worked in the petroleum industry in Canada. He researched alternative systems of government at Imperial College, London. He emigrated to Australia and was employed in mining development. He became a high school teacher and wrote science textbooks published by the Queensland Department of Education.

This book is his ninth novel published. He has been writing fiction novels full-time since 2013: speculative, love, politics, crime, sport, totalitarianism, science and satires. He is involved in public policy-making, has proposed an underground railway for Brisbane and a new paradigm for climate science. He discusses current issues at U3A and has studied philosophy with students at the University of Queensland. He attends community development forums.

He blogs views of ideas in his books and relates them to events in the news. He writes letters, plays the guitar, plays chess and walks in the park by the river where he lives.

He enjoys reading, watches movies and enjoys The Big Bang Theory.

He is divorced with children and grandchildren.

LIST OF NOVELS PUBLISHED

Available from Amazon in Australia, USA, UK and Canada

The Grass is Always Browner (2011)
Love Straddle (2014)
Presumed Dead (2018)
$hort of Love (2019)
Time is Gold (2020)
Animal Farm 2 (2021)
Turkeys not Bees (2022)
Brisbane River Anti-Memoir (2023)
The Camel, The Lion and The Child (2024)

A few passages have been extracted from previous books and included in this book without referencing

CONTENTS

	PART 1 ADOLESCENT SPIRIT		
1	Rocket	22	Peronism
2	Bully	23	Gringo Visit
3	Complaint	24	Ocean Spirit
4	Blowdown	25	Crew rights
5	Justice	26	Sail locker
6	Crossing the ditch	27	Storm
	PART 2 HERD AND DESERT	28	Idealism
7	Joining the herd	29	Capsized
8	Lab rats	30	Laid up
9	Totty		PART 5 DRAGON
10	Compliance	31	Imperial College
11	Acorn	32	Society game
	PART 3 CAMEL	33	Teesside
12	Slaves	34	Collision
13	Office rivalry	35	Dimorphic conflict
14	Spring break up	36	Patricide
15	Computer models		PART 6 CHILD
16	Brick delivery	37	Back at school
	PART 4 LION	38	Freedom writing
17	Galapagos		PART 7 IMMORTAL
18	Love in ruins	39	Reincarnation
19	Currency exchange	40	Cold War
20	Nationalism in Peru		EPILOGUE
21	New Australia		

MAIN CHARACTERS

Self Maidment — protagonist, a student, engineer, science teacher and writer

Gretchen — married to Self

Sarah — their daughter

Michael — their son

Vicki — a psychology student

Barbara — an office worker

Burke — Self's PhD supervisor

Superman — Self's alter ego

Maria — yacht crew member

PART 1
ADOLESCENT SPIRIT

Friedrich Nietzsche's book Thus Spake Zarathustra has a spirit, thirty years old, called Zarathustra, who in his prologue descends from the spirit world to live in the World of men. The descent is narrated as the fable of The Three Metamorphoses:

> 'how the spirit becometh a camel, the camel a lion, and the lion at last a child.'

Self was raised from a boy on a farm, a place different from the wilderness where Zarathustra's camel spirit hastened to and was transformed to a lion in the desert and then to a child. But Self's spirit was real and transcended in the same sequence as Zarathustra's, from camel, to lion, to child.

His parents had named their son Self, because he was a self-determined baby, becoming a self-contained child, quite independent, with a mind of his own.

As he grew, his awareness was of school homework, helping on the farm, training an excitable horse, contending with conflict at school, doing his homework and competing at sport. He was curious, questioning everything to find out causes and effects. His progress depended at first on teachers and supervisors. He was content to adopt the pace of his siblings and his peers, receiving mainly fair treatment. When he started at university, his spirit embraced freedom, challenges, responsibility and a new anonymity.

CHAPTER 1
ROCKET

If the horse his father gave him had been placid and obedient, Self's life would have been different. The wilful animal challenged him whenever he got into the saddle. He rode at weekends, by which time the horse would be bursting with pent up energy, dancing about and chafing at the bit. Both he and the horse developed to be excitable, determined and fiery. Their learning about each other was erratic and slow.

He first saw his horse when his father lowered the tailboard of the farm's cattle trailer and led him down. He had come from a horse sale at Bridgwater Fair. He was half Arab and half Welsh Hill Pony, with the characteristic concave Arab nose and arched neck. He was big, fourteen and a half hands, iron grey, a pretty horse, with a strong chest. Born on the local Quantock Hills, he ran with his mother and her mob for the first two years. The year before, when they separated out ponies to be sold, he was still suckling and had been passed over as too young to be sold off.

He hadn't seen many humans up close before and shied away from Self when he put out a hand to touch him. Self had in his pocket nubs of cow cake from the dairy and held one out on the flat of his hand. Gingerly, he took it.

He had a long bushy tail and a white star on his forehead. He was alert, with quick movements.

'I am going to call him Rocket,' Self said. 'He seems ready to take off.'

They both were beginners. Self was his first rider and Rocket was his first horse. His father hadn't trained a pony himself and may not have realised the cocktail he was mixing had a kick. The two fought for control. It was an unusual arrangement and Self wondered if his father was disappointed by his slow progress.

'You can break each other in,' his father said, as if the result had to be good, however long it took.

His parents had named him 'Self' because as a baby he was a free spirit, a delight when he was getting what he wanted, but horribly stubborn when he wasn't. His interest was primarily himself. His self-absorption became more pronounced as he got older. Psychometric surveys of adolescents have found they perceive their spiritual health to connect more to self than to Others, to Nature, or to Transcendence. As a teenager he liked to be in control, not showing his emotions, lacking empathy for others and preferring his own company.

The family name was Maidment. His name, Self Maidment, was an epithet suggesting autonomous creation and intention. Teachers and administrators usually asked him to spell it, as if it might mean something.

They wondered if Self would learn to be employable. His father had learned farming on-the-job, living in at the farmhouse. There he met a girl who became his wife and her father sponsored the tenancy of the large farm they took when they married.

They had four children and Self was third. His father was a successful farmer and supposed Self could learn to ride by going riding. In his view, controlling his horse would develop him for employment.

Self struggled to control Rocket. His father was surprised by the combat that ensued. He had wanted the pairing to toughen Self up, but the two seemed hell bent on destroying each other.

'I like it that you are still trying to control him,' his father said. 'You could have given up. Some horses can't be trained. There is no shame in quitting. I could find someone to buy him.'

'Why would anyone buy him?'

'They could want to train him.'

'I don't think anyone could.'

Self rode Rocket with difficulty. After a year of fighting to control him, one day he had ridden up to a farm gate made of tubular steel, with his father watching him from afar. He slid down, opened it and led Rocket through. Then he climbed back into the saddle and galloped him up a grassy farm track to a small hill a kilometre away. It was fast, exhilarating, with the wind roaring past his ears. The next gate was closed too but before he could climb down, Rocket bolted. He galloped at a furious pace back down the track, with Self holding on and pulling on the reins with all his strength and Rocket clenching the bit to hold it forward in his mouth, preventing control. As they neared the bottom of the hill, with the closed steel gate ahead, Self considered bailing out, but knew he would likely break something, so he hung on. He thought Rocket might slow down but he galloped at full speed into the steel gate, bending it. Self was thrown over the gate and lay immobile on the ground. Rocket began grazing as if nothing had happened.

'Are you alright?' his father asked, running up.

Self got slowly to his feet.

'I saw the whole thing,' his father said. 'You could have been killed. I ran and ran. That horse has a lot of wildness still in him. His spirit wants to escape. He will take a lot of taming yet.'

'I have tried to control him but he's too strong.'

'To control him, you have to master your own wildness first. You cannot let him gallop up a hill and then expect him to go quietly back down.'

'But I liked galloping up.'

'It isn't about what you like, it's about self-mastery, making what you want happen. Before you can tame him, you have to tame yourself. It's up to you to make something of that horse.'

Self climbed up into the saddle and rode him quietly back to the stable.

He knew that unwanted horses were bought by knackers, to be slaughtered to make dog food. It would be a tragedy. He realised he admired Rocket for what he was and had affection for him. He could not possibly quit and redoubled his efforts.

He was trying to control an animal bigger, heavier and stronger than himself. Ultimately he was powerless to stop him. Horses have minds of their own and a good rider has to be patient to work *with* an independent horse, not against him.

He worked hard at his schoolwork and the unremitting slog was relieved by riding. Self may have projected his own rebellious spirit into Rocket. When he was having difficulty at school, instead of fighting the school system, a stoush on Rocket was like releasing a safety valve. As he and Rocket tired, the ride became less combative and was sometimes pleasant.

Staying in control depended on keeping Rocket calm. His bolting could be dangerous, because he would charge into a closed iron gate without hesitating, throwing Self to the ground. Then he would gallop away, back to the stable. On one occasion, he galloped all the way along the roads back to his home on the hills, where he had lived as a foal. It took Self and his father a week of searching to find him. They enticed him with nubs of cake, slipped a halter on and Self rode him back to the farm.

By riding a lethally fast horse, Self's confidence grew, the same as the driver of a sports car develops bravado. He became ostentatious, where once he had been modest. He would gallop down the cobblestoned street of the local village. The clatter of Rocket's metal shoes echoed in the quietness of a Sunday morning and was probably attributed to wildness in Self's character.

'He's improving,' his father said. 'You are training him.'

It was a breakthrough. Self's ego expanded. Freud had described a horseman riding a strong wild horse, his instinctive id fearful, his superego guiding him to adopt external standards of morality and kindness, his ego trying to control the horse.

It was decided for him that Rocket would be castrated. Afterwards he was less antagonistic but at the same time less willing. When Self tried to anticipate his thinking, he was less successful, as if the horse had withdrawn from him a little and would not forgive him.

His intelligence became familiar to self, because he knew how he would respond in situations. Like Self, he had doubts and fears. Self supposed that Rocket's mind continually churned with possible actions, as did his own. He wondered if he would also think about more remote concerns, such as previous outings and the future.

The wonderful thing about horses is they want to be reliable and serve. Horses seldom try to harm their riders. Even when Rocket bolted, which could be dangerous, he kept his footing and didn't try to throw Self off. Self's most enjoyable riding was driving cattle or sheep between pastures. Rocket understood to follow behind the herd, when he would relax and he and Self would work together.

As he contemplated his schoolwork, preparing for eventual employment, Self's experience with Rocket had revealed to him that it was his own lack of understanding that was holding them back. Because learning was by trial and error, progress was abrasive and inefficient. By reflecting on his successes he slowly learned to control Rocket.

'Good,' said his father. 'He is more manageable every time you take him out.'

Despite not achieving conventional command of the horse, Self's riding was a valuable experience for him. Contending with a wilful strong animal, the stubbornness in his character was physically and mentally exercised by more conflict than he wanted. He learned to be strong, analytical and patient.

Rocket developed into an exciting ride for an experienced rider. When Self left home to go to university, Rocket was bought by elite Millfield School near the farm, for polo players to ride. Rocket's strength, speed and stamina were valuable in chukkas. It was a sad parting after exciting times together, a new beginning for both of them.

With good instruction, both could perform well.

CHAPTER 2
BULLY

From age 11 to 18, Self went to the local grammar school in Bridgwater. At first he aimed to please his parents, but in adolescence his spirit transformed to pleasing himself, most of the time. The transformation was punctuated by several profound and painful incidents, that set his values.

At school, he hung out with a group of his age-peers, the under-13s rugby team. They played fixtures with schools in nearby towns. At the end of the winter season, they were undefeated and morale was high. They dispersed in the summer to play cricket and compete at athletics. When the next school year started in September, the team reformed as the Under 14s. In the playground, Self and his team ruled over the new first formers.

The team's full back, Buller, was a swaggering boy who kicked conversions. Being in the year below, he wasn't a close friend of Self's. When the boys fooled around on the playing field during a morning tea break, Self noticed him bullying a first former, putting a leg behind him and slamming him down on the grass.

Self saw himself as protecting the small newcomers. He wanted to give Buller a taste of his own medicine and tripped him up. Caught unawares, Buller fell heavily and came up with his fists clenched. This was unusual, for fighting in the playground was done by wrestling, not by fist fighting. Usually the combatants tried to get each other in an arm lock or neck lock, grappling until one surrendered.

They were quickly surrounded by a ring of boys chanting:
'C'mon Maidment!'
'Give it to him, Buller!'

Each of the opponents had his own following. They were of similar size, used to the physicality of rugby. Self expected that the fight would be a close thing.

Self squared up to him, then Wham! Bam! Buller landed two punches, one in each eye, blinding him temporarily. That was the end of the fight. Shock, horror! Self had been defeated by a younger boy. He found out that Buller was learning boxing at the Police Boys Club, explaining his superior ability with his fists.

Self didn't get over his embarrassment. For three more years at school he played rugby alongside Buller, but they kept their distance. It was the last time Self fought anyone. He developed an abhorrence of fighting. He had realised that winning in a fight was not the way to resolve a difference honourably. There was a 'cold war' going on for years and he hoped he wouldn't have to fight.

Self opposed bullies when he could, from his experience of losing this fight at school. He had tripped Buller, which was bullying too. He had been in the wrong and he had paid a high price.

He had other opportunities at school to compete using his skills, on the playing field and in the classrooms - but the rules were sometimes unfair.

Self competed with his classmates in exams, trying to come top of the class. Schoolwork was an endless round of instruction, competition and evaluation. There was no formal system for rating teacher competence, but when a teacher was unfair, students protested by misbehaving.

His project in his 3rd Form woodwork class was a cross halving joint, to join two pieces of wood together at a right angle. Self worked carefully to cut and chisel the pieces to fit together precisely. He was pleased with the result and looked forward to being assessed. In most of his classes he was accustomed to coming near the top.

The teacher, Mr Jones lined them up, holding their joints. He stood them in a line, from top to bottom of the class, telling them where to stand.

'You, go in the middle,' he told Self.

It was unfair, but Self said nothing.

Jones was vehement and fierce, with a red face and veins on his nose.

'Next you!' he said to the boy next to Self. 'Go two down from the top.'

Self was outraged. The boy's joint had been cut badly and the fit was loose.

Jones put his favourite student in the top position, at the start of the line, although his work was nothing special.

'Jonesie isn't fair,' Self muttered to the boy beside him.

'Who's that talking?' Jones thundered. 'You know the rules, Maidment. No talking. Go to the bottom of the class.'

Self stood at the end of the line, holding the work he was proud of, humiliated and in despair.

At morning break, he was still angry and got into a fight. A prefect sent them to Jack, the Deputy Principal.

'What have you two got to say for yourselves?' Jack asked.

Neither said anything. Self knew a confession would be wussy.

'If you won't tell me, you can write it down. I want an essay from each of you, by tomorrow, saying what you like and what you don't like about this school. You can have six strokes apiece, to focus your thinking.'

Deputy Jack did all the caning and he was good at it. He bent Self over a table and hit him with a physics metre ruler six times. It hurt a lot but Self was quiet. His spirits sank to the lowest they had ever been. Maybe he would never try at schoolwork again.

He did the essay at home. He wrote that he liked to do his school work well and he didn't like it when a teacher marked him unfairly, as Mr Jones had done, putting him bottom of the class when his work was about the best. A boy in the school yard had jeered at his low assessment, making him angry.

Then he enlarged on his theme.

He wrote: 'Mr Jones throws wood chisels at students. He repairs lawn mowers in class time for cash. He gives the top marks to students who live near his home.'

Self's brother had told him about the mower repairs and knowing his brother, it was probably lies. He wanted Jack to know that Jones was crazy, as most students believed. Jones' disregard for objective assessment of student performance was abhorrent. He punished disrespectful student behaviour, rather than rewarding achievement at woodwork. Self's woodworking skill had been cancelled by his misdemeanour. It wasn't fair.

Self felt passionately that playing the man and not-the-ball was foul behaviour. He liked woodwork and wanted to register his belief that achievement depended on performance at woodwork alone. Misbehaviour resulted from incompetent teaching.

Next day, he handed his essay to Jack. Jack didn't read it while he was there. Self felt good having struck back. Not saying anything would have been pitiful. On the strength of his retribution, he began to feel better.

When he passed Jones in a corridor next day, the teacher stopped, glared at him and gave him a death stare. It seemed likely that Jack had told him of Self's accusations. Self was a rebel and it was heady having his complaint listened to, although he knew it was precarious. No-one said anything. He didn't know if anyone had read his complaints. Jones continued to give him death stares for the remainder of the year, until Self left woodwork.

CHAPTER 3
COMPLAINT

He was led into trouble by Jason, a boy of his own age who sat beside him on the school bus. Jason's twin brother Jude went to a different school. The twins had been separated by the 11-plus exam. Jason had passed and Jude had failed, despite having similar abilities. It would make a huge difference to their career opportunities. Jason's grammar school would send 50% of school leavers to university or to teacher training colleges, whereas most of Jude's secondary modern leavers went into trades, the best of them into apprenticeships.

The brothers were best friends and were lost without each other. The unfair separation affected their whole outlook. In First Form, Jason was merely aggrieved and petulant, but by the time he reached the Fifth, he had a chip on his shoulder and had grown into a violent thug. He refused to wear the school tie and cap despite being caned frequently. He did little school work and was relegated to the year group below Self's.

Self liked Jason and sympathised with his hostility towards the system. His family were bohemian and Self's mother forbade him to visit Jason. He copied Jason's disdain for the uniform and was caned several times. In Upper Sixth, all his class, except Self, were appointed prefects, resplendent in red-tasselled blue caps and able to lounge around in the prefects' room. Excluded from their company and slighted, Self was wretched.

His promotion could have been blocked because of his disobedience in not wearing the uniform, or by revenge wreaked by Jones. Self's association with Jason did not work in his favour. Jason was suspended for breaking a teacher's jaw. Jason was dangerous.

Self practiced javelin throwing with him, but refrained from aiming at the judges, as Jason sometimes did. He had a psychopathic tendency.

'Bet you I can throw the discus into the swimming pool,' he told Self.

'There are kids in there. You'll hit someone.'

'Too bad,' he replied.

Luckily he missed.

Jason was angry and he wanted Self to join in escapades. Then something good happened. Bill, his chemistry master, asked his son what was troubling Self. He was in Self's class and a friend. He told his father that Self was offended because he had not been made a prefect with the rest of them. Bill spoke up for Self and the Principal made Self a prefect. Bill was always kind to him, perhaps because Self was his keenest student. He felt good to belong again and to know there was justice in the world. It had taken sometime for justice to prevail, but he knew that if he stayed true to what he believed in, things would work out for him.

He longed to be older and free to live the way he wanted. He was confined by narrow adult values, unable to explore and discover his own.

Self learned the rules and standards of the education game. He learned to stand up for what he believed in, to be loyal to friends and behave responsibly. His adolescent spirit refocussed from obeying parents and teachers, or being led into trouble by Jason, to pleasing his inner self. When the rules were fair, he could succeed. Would the rules be fair in university and employment?

CHAPTER 4
BLOWDOWN

Self was accepted to study engineering at a redbrick university. He was one of a cohort of 80 freshmen with good A-level grades. He enjoyed studying and his diligence had earned high achievement in stiff competition. At university he worked in informal groups with friends, with less competition.

Self's first employment was as a science intern during the university vacation. He encountered the expectations of strangers and was surprised by their ambiguity. What they wanted him to do wasn't always obvious.

A large nuclear power station had been built at Hinkley Point, in Somerset, looming over the Maidment farm. Self's father was friendly with the station manager and asked him if he had work for Self for a couple of months in the university vacation. The manager said Self should write a letter to him, telling what he wanted.

He wrote that he was doing First Year Chemical Engineering at the University of Birmingham. He would be living at home after July 15th. The university wanted him to get practical experience during the vacation, relevant to his studies. Self wrote that he would be grateful if they would consider him for a position at the power station.

The lab manager, a Mr Arkhill, phoned him at the university and left a message for Self to call him back. He phoned and they talked.

'Would you be able to monitor water quality, collect samples and do tests?' Arkhill asked. 'The power station is large and nuclear powered, with a laboratory staff of 10 scientists. We monitor for any radioactive leaks, by testing samples of liquid and gas effluents. You could do some air quality testing between your water quality work. There isn't much chemical engineering though.'

Self said he was interested in radiation physics and it seemed ideal.

'I'm very interested,' said Self 'When can I start?'

They fixed a date and Self began paid employment. He collected samples of condensate from the turbine hall and brought them to the laboratory, where he measured oxygen contents with an electroanalytical test meter. He had to report high oxygen to the manager because it could cause corrosion and the condenser gas would have to be purged.

The lab manager told him an additional task was to check the chlorine content of seawater in the cooling circuit.

'Sea water, to cool the station's condensers, flows into a caisson offshore, entering a tunnel a kilometre long and two metres in diameter. Chlorine is injected at the inlet, to control growth of crustaceans inside the tunnel on the walls.'

Self checked and found chlorine was not being injected and he reported this to the laboratory manager.

'See if you can find out why the chlorine pump has stopped,' the lab manager ordered.

Self reported back to him.

'When I fiddled with it, it started.'

He had enjoyed his success with the chlorine system. He would like to do this work even without being paid.

Two hours later, there was a loud boom, shaking the glassware in the laboratory. The turbine hall was enveloped in a cloud of steam. Self thought it was a reactor meltdown and crawled under a bench in case there was ionising radiation.

'The condenser water tubes have been blocked by something,' a scientist said.

Just then the phone rang and the scientist answered.

'Fucking hell,' he said putting down the phone. 'The control room guys think we have blocked the condenser tubes with barnacles, so steam can't condense. They are blowing down the condenser to stop the turbines exploding.'

The scientist explained to him: 'Barnacles are filter feeders and the sea water flowing through the tunnel brings them food, creating an ideal environment for growth. We inject chlorine to stop them growing. The chlorine pump could have been down for weeks and nobody noticed. The barnacles could have built up on the walls. When you restarted the chlorine, they let go and were swept into the condenser manifold, blocking water entry to hundreds of cooling tubes. Without cooling water flowing, not enough heat could be taken away to condense the steam and the pressure built up, until the safety valve popped.'

The steam thundered out all afternoon until they shutdown the turbogenerator set.

'How can they remove the barnacles from the tubes?' asked Self.

'They will undo manually hundreds of bolts holding on the manifold covers. It will take a day or two.'

Self was in a controversial position. Not many people have caused a nuclear power station to shut down. But Self had done as Arkhill had told him and he was not in trouble.

'Did you have any idea of the havoc you would wreak by restarting the chlorine pump?' the lab manager asked him.

'No. I didn't know what the chlorine was for.'

'Well, you know now,' he said. 'How does it feel to have shut down a nuclear power station?'

'Not good.'

'It's not your fault,' the lab manager said. 'I should have known this would happen when I told you to find out what was wrong with the pump, but it had never happened before on my watch. I didn't realize the chlorine had been stopped for weeks. A lot of people are upset this happened.'

Self found there could be a different interpretation.

'The barnacles had to be cleared and there was no other way,' a scientist told Self. 'The barnacles had to be removed and the condenser would be blocked sooner or later. It was the failure of the chlorine pump that caused the problem.'

Self realised that the lab manager had been between a rock and a hard place.

'So a shutdown would have happened anyway?' said Self.

'Yes, probably,' the scientist said. 'Because he told you to find out what was wrong with the chlorine system, you're probably in the clear. He may have told his bosses that it was your fault. When something goes wrong, people try to distance themselves from blame.'

Self hadn't expected to encounter such ambiguity from strangers at his workplace. Checking the chlorine pump had not meant restarting it. He was supposed to leave it switched off. The instructions were vague. The manager could have wanted a fall guy to reduce his exposure to blame.

Fortunately for Self his employment at Hinkley Point had been protected by his father's friendship with the station manager. Self felt used. In future he would find out about the effects of his work and be able to take responsibility for his actions. If he had known the consequences beforehand, he might have varied what he did. For example, he could have warned the control room about the possibility of the condenser tubes becoming blocked.

His other learning from the internship was that a nuclear power station can only be as safe as its operators, who were only human and made mistakes. It was fortunate that no radioactive material had leaked.

There were other mistakes too. He assisted a science officer who was compiling a record of plant defects for the electricity generating company to make warranty claims against the construction company. For a week, Self lugged cameras, lenses and floodlights, to photograph defects. They photographed misaligned fittings, leaking pipes and vessels, cracked welds, burned out electric motors and faulty instruments. Some of the defects had potential for radioactive leaks. A few problems had arisen from unanticipated design problems and shoddy workmanship, but they had not been noticed until nuclear fission commenced. Other defects were discovered when operators reported problems. He became aware that a nuclear reactor is vulnerable to many types of human error.

A nuclear power station was an environment requiring special precautions against exposure to radiation and ingestion of radioactive substances. He wore a badge of unexposed photographic film on his lapel. It recorded radiation impacting it and was monitored weekly. If he was exposed above a certain level, he would be moved to a location with lower radioactive exposure and someone with lower exposure would be transferred in, to replace him. It didn't happen. But the system supposed jobs were interchangeable and Self heard a joke that no-one knew their job.

Self learned that his work as a technical person had required following the instructions of a responsible manager. Sometimes the manager did not know what had to be done and he followed the advice of experienced technical personnel. The manager had overall responsibility but Self was responsible for interpreting vague instructions correctly. Self's responsibility was to communicate and act in this problem-solving situation, overcoming ambiguity. It was challenging work and he realised he needed more experience. He had a lot to learn. Responsibilities were not defined and relationships with others depended on local experience, rather than regulations.

He had enjoyed the internship and learned a lot about personal responsibility when others were directing him. One thing he learned was not to ask questions that would make him responsible.

Chapter 5
Justice

After his vacation job at the nuclear power station finished, Self hitch-hiked with Nick, a university friend, to Italy for a month, before starting second-year. They were both 18. They made their way to Florence and then to Rome and Naples. They had only enough money to stay at youth hostels.

'There'll be a crowd out thumbing today,' Self said, as they set off from Naples to return to the UK.

At the autostrada entrance, hitch-hikers seeking rides were lined up. No-one stopped for them. Several pairs of girls alighted and were snapped up. A girl-boy couple were picked up.

'Nick, you could pass as a girl, if you fluff up your hair, point your toes and push out your chest and bottom,' Self joked.

'It's you that's unattractive, Self,' said Nick. 'We should split up. A driver might feel sorry for you.'

'F**k you,' said Nick.

They stayed together but no-one stopped for them.

'We might go better earlier in the day,' said Self. 'Let's go back into Naples and come back here tomorrow morning.'

It was a long walk into the city and they were footsore and despondent.

The next morning they began to make their way out to the autostrada again.

'If we use all our money, we can get a train past Rome,' said Nick.

'We will need money to get through Switzerland.'

'We'll cross our bridges when we come to them,' Nick said.

'Tunnels could be difficult.'

'Look at all these cars,' said Nick. 'Perhaps a driver will take us if we ask?'

'Getting pushy won't work,' Self said. 'Drivers prefer to do the asking,'

'Let's look for a car with keys in it and borrow it,' Nick said.

'We're not that desperate.'

'University commences next Monday,' said Nick. 'We're already late. It will take until then to get back by thumbing.'

'Okay. Let's look for a car,' said Self. He had never stolen a car before and his thinking couldn't imagine serious consequences. It would be just to borrow a car standing idle to help their education.

Taking opposite sides of the road, they began scouting along lines of parked cars, looking for one with keys in the ignition.

'Hiya Guys!' said a confident American voice. 'Are you staying locally?'

'No. We're trying to get back to the UK, for university,' said Self, hoping he hadn't seen what they were doing.

'How are you travelling?'

'Hitch-hiking. Trying to,' Nick said.

'I guess it isn't easy. I might be able to help you. I'm leaving this afternoon to drive to Germany. Would you guys like a ride?'

They couldn't believe their luck.

'I'm a doctor at an American army base in the Ruhr. It'll be a comfortable ride. I'm driving a Mercedes convertible.'

It seemed perfect. 'Thank you,' they said.

'Now, before we go, would you like a feed?' he asked.

They hadn't eaten a meal for days.

'There's a place just along here where I can shout you some pasta or something.'

'Thank you very much.'

They tucked into plates of spaghetti bolognaise and it seemed to be working out fine. Their host sat with them as they ate.

'I'll go and get my car now,' he said. 'It's at a garage around the corner. They're taking out a ding. When I get it, we'll leave for Germany.'

He went out. A few minutes later he came back.

'There's a small problem,' he said. 'They want cash and I'm a bit short. The banks are closed until tomorrow. Say, do you guys have a hundred dollars in lira I can borrow until Monday? About 200,000 Lira? I'll go to a bank along the way and give it back first thing tomorrow.'

It was most of the money they had, but they lent him what he wanted. They wouldn't need money until Germany, which was close to home. They were suspicious, but questioning him could upset him and lose their ride.

'Okay?' he asked.

They nodded dumbly and he left. They never saw him again and he left them with the bill for the spaghetti. The restaurant owner made them wash dishes.

They told their story at the British Consulate, but the official knew the situation well.

'Then he left with your money and didn't come back?'

'Yes.'

'This situation is quite common here. There's nothing we can do. Put it down to experience.'

Self and Nick took three days to hitch-hike to the UK, arriving starved and exhausted. They never found out if they had been taken down by an American, or by an agent of the Italian police who had seen them trying to steal a car. Either way, it was salutary experience. Afterwards, Self realised how gullible they had been. It was lucky that they had been diverted from stealing a car, or the consequences could have been much worse. Perhaps they had received as much justice as they deserved.

CHAPTER 6
CROSSING THE DITCH

Halfway through second year, Self and four engineering student friends took part in a university rag stunt for fun. They modified an old family car, fitting paddle wheels to cross the English Channel, as a highlight of rag week, a traditional festival, as a stunt to attract publicity and donations to charities.

The five had different roles. Larry publicised their venture in city newspapers. A reader donated an old Vauxhall Velox car. He arranged with the head of the Chemical Engineering Department, Professor Davies, for alumni engineering businesses to fabricate steel floats and paddle wheels and for the students to access the department's workshops. A donor supplied a painter to emblazon the university coat of arms on the bonnet. Another alumnus provided truck transport to Dover.

The team worked in a university workshop bay used for constructing chemical engineering pilot plants.

'Is this chemical engineering, or did I miss something?' someone asked.

'We are using a chemical fuel to power paddles and overcome fluid friction,' Self replied. 'There is chemical engineering everywhere.'

Previously, their innovations had been individual, without experience or skills in common. It was novel to meet formally, to decide responsibilities and agree a design for a paddle car. Reaching a reasoned design by group discussion was a challenge.

They each had separate responsibilities, with Larry managing overall and coordinating joint aspects. Self designed long cylindrical floats and helped Nick weld them to the car, making a catamaran. He designed paddle wheels as extensions of the rear axle. Mart inserted a second gearbox in the car's drivetrain, so the paddle wheels would turn at the right speed. Maciek created publicity with his photographs and graphic images.

Self taught himself to weld by trial and error. When his vision was obscured by near-opaque welding goggles, he had difficulty seeing to strike arcs. Ignoring safety warnings, he stopped wearing the goggles and was temporarily blinded.

'Self, you are an idiot.'

'I tried to help with the welding,' Self said. 'I didn't know I wouldn't be able to see what I was doing.'

With his eyes inflamed and painful, they took him to a hospital. His retinas had almost detached. He was laid up for two weeks. There wasn't much he could do, wearing sunglasses, waiting for his eyes to heal. After that, he observed safety precautions assiduously.

They tested the craft in a canal basin near the university. It almost sank, because instead of using the formula for the volume of a cylinder: $\pi r^2 L$, to calculate the floats' displacement, Self used: $2\pi r L$, which was the surface area, a lesser amount. When they tested it in a local canal, the floats were too small and it almost submerged. They solved it by cutting off the back end of the car. Self was embarrassed by his error and never relied on his memory to recall formulae again.

As if the floats fiasco wasn't bad enough, Self's paddle wheels produced less speed than he had hoped for. Self learned that his intuitive designs needed to be carefully checked. Larry borrowed a pair of outboard motors, in case the channel current proved too strong for the paddles. But they continued to use the paddle wheels, with the throaty roar of the unmuffled car engine more aesthetic than the purr of the outboards.

They rode to Dover in the truck with the car, followed by carloads of supporters, launched it and set off for Calais accompanied by an escort boat, for safety and photography. The paddle car bobbed over the waves, as if a family had driven to the coast on holiday and continued on into the sea. They looked out through the windscreen as they slid down a swell, climbed up the next one and bobbed over.

It took them about seven hours to make the crossing. The tide swept them up the Channel to Belgium. They came back hours later, scrambling to enter Calais harbour, narrowly averting being swept down the channel to the ocean beyond.

Later the same day, they were tired and thankful to set off for Dover with the escort boat towing their craft. A storm blew up and the pitching of the escort boat broke the tow line. It was too risky to reattach a line to the drifting steel catamaran.

News and photos of their feat were in the British newspapers. A parliamentarian at Westminster questioned why university students, their studies publicly funded, had left a family car on a steel platform adrift in the busiest shipping channel in the world. If it collided with an oil tanker, he said, an oil spill could destroy tourist beaches and fisheries on both sides of the channel. The fear was real, because the raft was heavy and constructed rigidly from iron girders. It could punch a hole in an oil tanker.

Newspaper editorials criticised irresponsible students, but some applauded their initiative. The RAF was assigned the task of sinking it by dive bombing, but embarrassingly, they missed. There was a rumour it had floated into Boulogne harbour near Calais, where it was lifted out by a crane and placed in a playground for children.

The intrepid five returned in glory to Birmingham University, where they were feted by peers who, lacking the 'can do' spirit, hadn't stepped outside their everyday routines.

The team's bravura didn't come from nowhere. It was inspired in the tradition of their countrymen, who revere the 'ditch', which had kept away the Spanish Armada and thwarted Hitler. Adventurous university students were accustomed to crossing by swimming, rowing, walking with floats on their shoes and pedalling small planes. Rather than trivialising the crossing, these attempts illustrated that Britain was an island of hardy innovative seafarers.

Self saw himself as an engineer, a discipline that cultivated change. The stunt was a pioneering venture that had escaped the purview of regulating authorities in the past, although the same lassitude was not likely in future.

The relationship with the French was sometimes ambiguous. When they arrived in Calais, Nick was the first to leap ashore.

'I'll get breakfast,' he said, scrambling up a ladder to the quay.

He returned to where they were waiting empty-handed, with a long face.

'What happened?' Self asked him.

'I couldn't get anything,' he said. 'The bastards speak French.'

He wasn't serious. The Anglo-French Concorde project was underway and took off two years later. What would the crazy English do next?

Few students had used their time as creatively and imaginatively as team members. For Self, this project had been his first opportunity to exercise his 'can do' spirit in public. He had outgrown his role at home on the farm. He had glimpsed the power of industrial leadership at the power station and knew that he wanted to join the engineering 'herd'. It was his first experience of teamwork outside his family and he was encouraged that he had been accepted and could contribute. It was responsible involvement with practical engineering.

For the five of them, it was a first experience of teamwork beyond school sport. Communicating and taking responsibility had new challenges to rise to. There were tensions and friction but Larry's management was masterful and steadying.

Gradually Self found answers to questions about what career he should follow. He realised that he was good at chemical engineering and in a job as a chemical engineer he could expect to be safe, treated justly and remunerated fairly. He had known from the start of the course that he was intensely interested in chemical engineering and now it was his best prospect.

He was thrilled. He loved chemical engineering. He was going to become a chemical engineer. It was an epiphany, a breakthrough insight into an adult world with jobs, travel, careers, even marriage and children. There had been uncertainties hanging over him, that now seemed favourably resolved for the present. He would finish the course exhibiting all the excellence he could muster.

Their involvement in the stunt had been voluntary, but a year later they would be doing projects in their jobs and it was a transition to conditions in paid employment. The experience of successful innovation, attention to detail and team working was formative and buoying.

PART 2
HERD AND DESERT

Self was ambitious and wanted to emulate the glittering career of Isambard Brunel, who in the 19th century engineered designs for many railways, tunnels, bridges and ships. Self began as an acolyte in the herd of graduate engineers recruited by Canadian oil companies. They met at meetings of professional engineering associations.

There were other professionals: accountants, scientists, medics and psychologists, in the herd migrating on the corporate advisory savannah. The professions were like guild unions, requiring members to have minimum qualifications. They obeyed a Hippocratic Oath, or equivalent, whereas engineers did not have a 'do no harm' convention in their closed shop. Errors of commission were inevitable in engineering and less sinful than omission. Engineers operate on inanimate systems, sometimes with unknown consequences. When something doesn't work, they can try again.

Because engineers take more risks, arguably they need more courage, bordering on recklessness.

Self adopted Ayn Rand's philosophy of personal selfishness.

'It's the hardest thing in the world—to do what we want. And it takes the greatest kind of courage.'

Nietzsche taught people to engineer their lives. He likened the other people to a herd, indifferent to his teaching. The herd animals do not wish to carry and simply want safe and abundant pasture:

quietness, no surprises and a relatively wealthy life. They don't take risks and rely on the shepherd to guide them. They are like slaves.

The desert contained the herd, holding it together for protection from predators. Sustenance was sparse and the herd migrated to new pastures to have sufficient food. Self had first to learn to be an ordinary member of the herd. Once he had been accepted by the herd, he could attain a prestigious role.

CHAPTER 7
JOINING THE HERD

As a teenager, Self laboured in the farm's fields, barns and animal sheds. It was physical work that complemented the mental demands of his school work. It was mostly unpaid, but as he got older, his father gave him ten pounds weekly after hay making and again after the grain harvest.

The farm workforce was led by his father and brothers. A handful of farm workers lived with their families in farm cottages. His brothers left school after fifth form, to work on the farm, whereas Self stayed on for sixth form. His mother and two sisters ran the farm house.

'Self, your brothers are learning to be farmers. Your sisters can go to university or to business college, if they don't find husbands first. We can't afford to set you up in farming too,' his mother said.

'What will I do?' he asked her.

'You will have to get a job in Bridgwater, or if you do well at school, you could go to a university, or a teacher training college.'

Self asked his father what he should do.

'Nay lad, I don't know ought about studyin'. I left school when I was fourteen and worked in the fields. If you learn a profession, you could be better off than you would going farming. I could try to get you in as an apprentice at the farm machinery agency in Bridgwater. They want mechanics and fitters. Would that interest you?'

'I don't know.' He wasn't interested in anything.

'See how you get on with your schoolwork, lad. You'll find out what you're good at soon enough.'

Self's farm work was mainly milking cows, feeding animals, carrying bales and tractor work. In the summer school holiday, he worked with one or two others in a team all day, sitting in the field to eat a harvest tea brought from the farm house: ham sandwiches, with mustard and apple pie, washed down with sweet tea. He worked hard in the open on practical tasks with health benefits and the satisfaction of contributing to the family.

He was one of four children and quite inconspicuous except for his toil, which helped to make their farm a success. In the evenings in winter, in the hour or so between supper and bed, before they had a television set, the seven of them sat in the kitchen, lit by a kerosene lamp, listening to comedy serials on the radio: 'The Navy Lark', 'Beyond Our Ken', the only sound being creaking of chairs, sighs, coughs and chuckles.

His life was not uncomfortable, but his life seemed to be on hold. He was waiting for new experiences. Everything he did he had done before.

In summer, he played tennis each week with a group of friends and afterwards sank a couple of pints at the pub, wobbling home on his bicycle. His brothers went to day release classes locally and learned farming skills. They gained understanding of new technologies and animal husbandry techniques.

Self sometimes helped deliver a calf too large for the birth canal. Local lore was that if a calf was stuck, it had to be pulled away quickly, or it would asphyxiate. Self came across a magazine article contradicting this, saying if the umbilical cord was delivering blood and oxygen to the calf, speed was unnecessary. The cow could rest until she gathered strength to push it out. Self's book-learned information sometimes clashed with tradition and he was regarded as academic and suspect. When he was at university, his information on substantive issues was resisted and a rift developed between him and the family.

The farm operated with efficient routines. Breakfast was eggs and bacon at 9.00 am. Afterwards, tasks were allocated and they joined worker groups setting off for the various workplaces. His father usually went to the centre of activity, a field to be harvested, or a herd to be mustered for separation of animals for sale. Everyone knew their jobs and his father coordinated. The workers were proud of their farm and did their work carefully.

In a cornfield, there could be a combine harvester, several tankers taking the grain to the silo beside the farmhouse, a swather spinning the straw into rows, a baler packing and tying it, and several wagons carrying bales to a Dutch barn. The field would be a hive of industry and when the work had been done, everyone moved on to the next field. Harvesting lasted a couple of weeks, longer if the weather was wet.

Self liked to ride on the combine harvester as it scooped up and swallowed a river of standing ears on stalks, spewing a torrent of golden grains into a tanker alongside, ejecting a stream of smashed up straw from its rear.

His father supervised unobtrusively. He would walk a field being harvested, talking to a driver here, adjusting a machine there and tidying up any grain accidentally left standing. 'Faffing about' is how his father described what he was doing; he was modelling the high standard of efficiency he expected. Self tidied up too, like his father. The workmen followed his lead, were careful with their machines, wasted little of the crop and coordinated with each other to bring in the harvest profitably. Self learned from his father how to supervise workers, by enabling them to question and understand the work.

His brothers gave the workmen more orders than his father did. Self learned that workers do not like to be closely supervised, without freedom to exercise their own judgement. If they were given assignments with too many instructions, it could be stressful for them. They enjoyed doing a task in their own way, sometimes ignoring his brothers' orders.

His father usually worked near Self as he laboured, seldom directing and often advising. He helped Self lift heavy sacks of grain, by linking hands with him. Self never normally touched his father, except to shake hands with him, balking at the physical intimacy. Holding his father's rough and calloused hand embarrassed Self, revealing the reality of his arduous labour for his family.

They used a mechanical conveyor sometimes and Self developed an interest in mechanisation. He improvised a machine for screening grain. He decided to train as an engineer and worked hard at school to get the grades required to be accepted at university.

Learning on the farm helped Self join the workforce. His experience of work and supervision was valuable when he became an engineer.

Self learned from his father to make the most of things, fit in with others and improve opportunities for everyone. His father helped with the landlord's shoot, raising pheasants and organising shooting parties for the laird and his wealthy friends. He could easily have resented the posh Londoners, down for the weekend, inveterate snobs with little real feeling for the countryside and ignorant of the shooting tradition that went back hundreds of years.

His father collected pheasants' eggs from wild nests and sat them under bantams. Foxes, squirrels, jays and other vermin would have taken a heavy toll, but he penned them in protective coops in fenced woodland clearings, shooting predators that penetrated or lurked. The young birds fed on corn seconds, small and shrivelled grains, carried into the woods from the farm. They grew quickly and when they could fly, he released them to populate the woodland rides and brakes.

When Self was home from university, he was a beater for shooting parties, walking in a line with gun dogs, going through woods, putting up birds to fly ahead towards a line of gunmen downwind. There would be whoops and shouts, with staccato gunfire and the yelps of retrievers on the scent of fallen birds. At the end of a day's shooting, 15 guns sometimes had brought down 150 pheasants.

His father was an unpaid gamekeeper who enjoyed walking over his neighbours' land, with a gun under his arm, working his labrador, taking home at the end of the day a brace of pheasants for Sunday lunch. His pleasure was to ponder the eternal mystery of which coverts held birds and in what direction they would burst out when the beaters reached them.

At the start of the season, young pheasants ran up to the gunmen looking for food. One option was to ignore them, another to frighten them to fly up and shoot them. Self preferred they live for another day, with a sporting chance and let them slip by him, scurrying away through the undergrowth.

It seemed callous to view shooting as a sport, but he agreed with his father that the birds died quickly and if the woods were emptied of birds, as they would be by poachers without the penal deterrence of magistrates who were shooters, the trees and bushes where they lived would be cleared away and planted to crops. Losing the woodlands would diminish the variety of vegetation and wildlife that lived there. He was content to roam through the woods in his humble role as a beater, enabling others to enjoy themselves.

'There's worse things than pheasant shooting,' his father said. 'Those who would stop field sports don't understand that without them, wild animals would disappear.'

CHAPTER 8
LAB RATS

After second year, Nick and Self went to vacation jobs in an oil refinery in Montreal, Canada, arranged by Nick's father. Their parents paid the fares to Boston and they caught the bus up through New England, travelling under maple trees arrayed in their yellow, gold and orange livery.

The Laboratory Manager, Francois Dumas, was an old friend of Nick's father. He taught them to take gasoline samples from product pipelines and test them for concentrations of volatile hydrocarbons in the laboratory, using a gas chromatograph.

'If volatiles are insufficient, the gasoline won't ignite in engines,' manager Dumas told them. 'If you measure a sub-spec sample, call the control room immediately, so that the batch can be reprocessed.'

In the laboratory, they analysed the samples. The work wasn't much related to engineering and perhaps that's why it soon became tedious. It wasn't ideal vacation employment but Montreal was vibrant and they met locals who showed them the city.

Every day they printed out a report with their laborious results, but no-one seemed interested. After several weeks, they had not found any sub-spec gasoline and their work seemed pointless.

'There's no lack of volatiles.' Self said. 'It's summer and cold starts aren't going to be a problem until winter.'

They cut corners, taking samples from convenient locations, rather than from where they had been told. Their testing was slipshod, not bothering to flush out the equipment between samples.

'What we are doing is meaningless,' Nick said. 'No-one gives a tinker's cuss about our findings. They wouldn't know the difference if we used the same sample for every test, saving ourselves the sweat of collecting and testing them.'

Self felt guilty, knowing they should do the job properly.

'If we don't measure variation, they could become suspicious,' he said. 'We have to produce an analysis for every sample.'

'If we fiddle with the chromatograph display, we can get many analyses from one sample,' said Nick. 'No-one will ever know.'

It would be blatant cheating. Self wanted to live honestly.

'We should do what we agreed to do,' he said.

Nick was blasé. 'C'mon, Self. Wouldn't you rather read a book, than waste your time with this shit?'

Reluctantly Self agreed. They concocted credible analysis reports and reclined in armchairs in the general manager's office, reading and snoozing.

One night they arrived at the laboratory and were surprised to find the manager waiting for them.

'Would you come with me,' he said.

They followed him into his office. He kept them standing. Something was wrong.

'What happened last night?' he asked, looking from one to the other, suspiciously.

'Nothing unusual,' Self shrugged. 'Why?'

'A heating element in the main fractionating column burned out about midnight,' Dumas told them. 'The product was sub-spec. It should have been recycled and rectified. Instead, a large slug of gasoline was piped to Chicago and another loaded into a lake tanker. Several trainloads have gone west and the remainder has been trucked to service stations all over Ontario. The fault was not recognised until 9.15 am when the switchboard was jammed with customers complaining their vehicles wouldn't start. The fuel had too few volatiles. We are recalling the entire delivery. As we speak, there are hundreds, even thousands, of service station mechanics draining and refilling vehicle gas tanks across Canada and America. Some customers will never trust this company again. Your job was to find out this problem while it was here at the refinery. What happened?'

Nick and Self looked at each other and shrugged.

'We don't know.'

'Did you get any off-spec analyses?'

'No.'

'Now, tell me exactly where you got the samples from.'

They admitted faking the sampling, everything. They hadn't realised their results were used for anything and they were sorry. They hung their guilty heads.

Dumas' voice had an edge that would cut glass. 'I told you when and where to get the samples and you cheated. I told you the control room wanted to hear about off-spec results, but you thought you knew better and that there couldn't be any. You didn't do your work. Normally, I would fire you both. However, Nick's father is a mate of mine. I feel sorry for him, that he has a son like you. I'm giving you another chance. Remember this: I trusted you and you let me down. I am very unpopular around here just now and it's your fault. Get out of my sight, you lazy cheating smart-asses.'

Self was embarrassed. Nick had led him astray but that was no excuse. He had allowed himself to be led. He had behaved immaturely, ratting on his obligations. It wouldn't happen again.

'We are fortunate Dumas knows your old man,' Self told Nick.

'Do you think so?' Nick said. 'Dumas is sure to tell him and he will go mad at me.'

'We're no longer kids,' Self said. 'Your old man's anger is less than we deserve for this. Would you have wanted the company to sue us for fraud?'

'No.'

Now, years later the incident still haunted him.

'Do you think our cock up at the oil refinery rebounded onto your father?' Self asked Nick one day.

'He lost his job later that year,' Nick said. 'Shit.'

'It could have been our fault, after he had obtained those jobs for us,' Self said. 'How ungrateful we were. I want to live virtuously.

According to Aristotle, honesty is halfway between habitual lying and hubris.'

'We aren't habitual liars,' Nick said. 'I'm not sure how close we came to hubris.'

'Very close,' Self said. 'When people have asked me what I think of my work, I have told them science is honest and good. But we cheated. I know that my 'honesty' was faked, boastful and ugly. It was hubris.'

'Worse, it was hypocrisy!' said Nick.

Nick had persuaded Self to take part in the ruse, but he couldn't blame him. They had led each other on.

They would learn from this incident to comply with normal expectations of herd workers who normally did tasks, not always because they understood the rationale, but because they respected others' expectations. A condition of acceptance in a herd is that an individual respects other members. They would want to be a part of the herd, cooperating, competing in only a few activities, having the herd protect them. Without protection by the herd, if they were weak or straggled, predators could hunt them down. They could be shut out by the union, lose their jobs, or even lose their lives.

'We had an obligation to the other workers to do our work. We never thought of that,' said Self. 'Many people serve their community loyally day after day, year after year, making the effort to do their tasks, without knowing their purpose or consequences.'

'That is what they are paid to do.'

'We were paid, but it wasn't enough,' said Self. 'We wanted to have our work acknowledged too.'

'It was ego tripping,' said Nick. 'We sat in the manager's chair feeling like big men.'

'We were very small,' said Self. 'The smallest workers in the herd.'

Self wanted to be respected by his peers more than anything. Being one of the group meant a lot. They would applaud his successes, laugh when he fooled around and comfort him when he made mistakes. By cheating, faking his work and bludging, he had let them all down. Manager Dumas would suspect every one of them of capability and intent to do the same thing and he would tighten his control. The group had lost his trust and they were no better than the wild herd of workers outside. Self and Nick were nothing special and they knew it.

They returned from Montreal to begin the third and final year of their engineering course.

They reflected on their career prospects.

'I don't want work that is routine, like sampling and analysis,' Nick said. 'I want to take pride in what I do.'

'What's wrong with sampling and analysis?'

'It's so boring it eats me up on the inside.'

'You probably think I'm wild,' Self said. 'But I want to live my life with courage. Nelson Mandela said *'Courage is not the absence of fear, but the triumph over it. The brave man is not he who does not feel afraid, but he who conquers that fear.'*

'Mandela had a cause to fight for,' said Nick. 'Do you?'

'I want to confront something that threatens everyone's future and can be overcome by reason and strength.'

'The future has plenty of threats,' said Nick. 'Which one are you going to overcome?'

'I want to solve the Cold War,' Self said.

'Wow! That's ambitious.'

'Unless I go out on a limb, I am never going to reach the best fruit,' Self said. 'I want to get to the most worthwhile risks, with the biggest prizes. It won't get any easier by waiting fearfully, dying slowly.'

'I don't think you'll find much risk as a scientist you can take on,' said Nick. 'From what I have seen, scientists like to choose the common denominator having least risk and run with the herd.'

'That's not fair,' Self replied. 'Sometimes scientists avoid dealing with problems of human behaviour, ethics, politics and economics, because they lack confidence or feel unqualified. Going against the herd takes courage.'

'I agree,' said Nick. 'Scientists don't normally take risks. If you are going to stick your neck out, the herd will be against you. You will need all your courage.'

'The herd tries to control us. Bertrand Russell once said:

'Collective fear stimulates the herd instinct and tends to produce ferocity towards those who are not regarded as members of the herd.'

'Risk taking is unwelcome in workplaces,' said Nick. 'When we were young, our experimenting was tolerated and we were protected. Now we have to conform. Forget about running against the herd: your plan is dangerous. People pursue their ambitions gradually, when opportunities arise. Declaring commitment to a paradigm shift invites opposition.'

'Having courage is when you overcome timidity by mustering many small acts of defiance into a single act of resistance,' Self said.

'You will be out on a limb,' said Nick.

'According to Helen Keller, Life is either a daring adventure or nothing at all,' Self said.

'Without sight or hearing, she became an author, disability rights advocate, political activist and lecturer.'

'Do you want to be that daring?' said Nick. 'Oh, you crazy wonderful person.'

CHAPTER 9
TOTTY

When they commenced third year, Self and Nick were feeling confident they could attract girlfriends for their final year of study. The end was in sight and their mate-attracting prospects were good. In first year, the university girls had ignored them and the only partners available for dancing, kissing and bedding were girls from outside: nurses, teachers and office workers. Males at the university outnumbered girls, but on Saturday evenings hundreds of girls minced in for dances., called 'hops', held in the students' union and a temporary gender balance was achieved.

Gulls flock to be safe from predators. Although the girls aspired to be distinctive, they felt safest with their own kind and flocked to the hops. Girls tottered in on platform soles, earning the name 'totty'. They all wore the same clothes, hair in the same style and talked about the same topics. The savannah was bare of variety and they all moved together, keeping respectful distances, forming a common front against predators.

There were loud bands playing for three dance floors packed with students, known pejoratively as a 'cattle market'. It was a herd experience, with much pushing, little opportunity to talk, a cultural desert. Females engaged socially to maximise their attractiveness and to get access to the highly rated males, with prospects and reputations for sophisticated dealing with highly rated women.

University girls never went to hops. Self's girl friend was an arts student. The two of them went to movies or spent evenings kissing.

In second year, Self dated university girls but he was unable to obtain the steady relationship he wanted. He dated a psychology student who lived in a hall next to his. They usually had a party to go to. When their kissing tapered off and she wouldn't go on a date with him, he found an office worker, Barbara, to have sex with.

To join the herd of engineers, undergraduates like Self and Nick would be on probation. To gain the anonymity in the herd they desired, they would have to suffer several years of laboratory testing and monitoring work, or equivalent,. It was dehumanizing, like preparing to cross a desert.

There didn't seem to be any alternative than to commence a career with a long apprenticeship. The work Self most wanted required striving, bringing autonomy and happiness, like climbing a mountain, within reach. To control herd conditions as an individual, getting job satisfaction, he would have to wait.

Self was recruited to work for a company in Canada, conditional on gaining a good degree. He spent most of the year working, except for sex breaks with his office worker girl.

Self seldom helped his brothers with their work on the farm them now. His family had no objections to him going abroad. If they had objected, he would have gone anyway.

Self distinguished himself with a first class honours degree, one of three awarded in the cohort of 80 students. It attracted offers of postgraduate work and employment. It was the first time his role in the herd had ceased to be anonymous. It was good to be recognised as a high achiever but there was jealousy too. Some old friends withdrew from him, as if his company threatened their competence.

He wanted to make a clean break away from his office worker girlfriend but there were complications. Their relationship was mostly sexual and he didn't want to take it further or make a commitment. He had told Barbara months earlier he was going to a job in Canada. She had continued going with him, knowing he was leaving. Instead she tried to hold him by inveiglement, which turned out unpleasant for everyone. He wanted to fade away into the herd but she wanted to go with him, as if this was her right. He was years away from settling down with a partner for life. He wanted to finish with her, but he postponed breaking it off until he finished at the university and had packed to travel to Canada.

He had told her that he wanted to separate but she wanted him to take responsibility for her, as if he had an obligation to her, which did not resonate with him sufficiently to change his plan to go alone. Her grief saddened him but their relationship had reached a crossroads and he lacked interest to go on together, because it would be a default option in which he would be compromised by a relationship fatally flawed by his lack of commitment.

Self left England to go to Canada under a cloud. Barbara's parents thought he had misled her, that their relationship would be permanent. It had lasted for a year and a half, but Self had been preoccupied with study and they had shared little other than a bed. She knew that he didn't want to spend his life with her, or anyone else. He was going to Canada alone.

CHAPTER 10
COMPLIANCE

Self was one of a cohort of young engineers who joined Continental Oil at their Calgary office. They blended into the company's herd of engineers, zealously pursuing their fortunes individually, respecting experience and not overtly competing with each other.

His life revolved around his work, often socialising with workmates out of office hours. He skied, played rugby, flew, swam, camped, ate, drank and partied with them, enjoying similar tastes in travel, women and cars.

Continental Oil Limited had recruited him as a petroleum engineer. He attended an elite reservoir school at the parent company's research centre in Houston. He was indoctrinated in the company's catechism of methods for evaluating petroleum resources. There were engineers from all over the World there and it was exciting to be at the cutting edge of a global technology.

When he returned to Canada, he spent three months of 'orientation' at each of several provincial offices. He became familiar with the organisation's terrain and was able to propose technologies that could increase production efficiency, but he was usually regarded as too young and his ideas were not considered seriously.

The workplace was dominated by middle-aged engineers with PhDs, who were there on secondment from the parent company in the US occupying management positions. Their technical prowess was in esoteric proprietary math, inaccessible to Self. Their arcane math logic set a tone like a monastery: devoid of colour and creativity, without intellectual discussion of ultimate purposes of the work. They often ignored Self's input. The inherited culture was that herd members put in the required hours, took their pay, holidays and superannuation, without imagining they had choices.

The routine work had little variety and was of little intrinsic interest to Self. His role was to adopt working methods assigned to the group, moving with the herd, preventing accidents by avoiding unnecessary risks and respecting authorities. It was usual to have a team supervisor bring together the different expertises. They worked in an open plan office area and overlooked each other's work.

Because he was only 21, age was a barrier. He despaired that unless he married, he would be held down to menial work until age 30. He was being passed over because he was single, while others less able were preferred. Marriage would enable him to move up the hierarchy sooner.

He was allocated a desk sharing an office with a middle-aged geologist who explained to him the company's methods for describing oil reservoirs. He answered Self's rookie questions and the two became friendly. His new office companion swigged milk all day.

'I have an ulcer,' he said. 'It could kill me. It's my nerves.'

He was off sick for weeks at a time.

He gave Self career advice.

'Take it easy or you'll end up with an ulcer like mine.'

Self was habitually anxious, unable to relax as he struggled to conform. It was oppressive and he began getting stomach pains. They changed him to another office, sharing with a young engineer in his starting cohort. He was a dull, pedantic person, with his father on the board of directors of Continental Oil. The son's engineering was largely social, his talk on the telephone inane. His loud and boring voice irritated Self. He was 'hale fellow well met' with the guys at the office, whereas Self's concentration prevented banter and socialisation.

The others were in awe of Self's first class honours degree and they froze him out. Pairing him to share an office with a bore, seeming like management manipulation to make Self more conforming and his companion more competitive. But it had the opposite effect, creating hostility and making Self feel ill. He went to a doctor, who asked him who he worked with. He told him of his antipathy towards his office companion.

'His popularity makes me anxious and envious,' Self told the doctor. 'That's when I get stomach pains.'

'You seem to be very competitive,' the doctor said. 'Stop worrying about your work. You need to collaborate. Your education has individuated you and now you need to stop competing and take part in community living. Unless you stop worrying, it will kill you.'

This sombre prognosis came as a shock to Self and he felt like a mindless drudge running on a corporate hamster wheel of exertion. His health was affected by endless churning of his frustrated thoughts pointlessly at home. He was anxious about his future, about his failures and others' successes, but he didn't know what he could do differently. Making friends was difficult. He put his head down and worked as hard as he could, hoping things would improve.

Rigours of adolescence and naivety notwithstanding, his spirit survived. Gradually he was accorded a place in the anti-intellectual engineering herd for his next assignment.

CHAPTER 11
ACORN

He was transferred to Continental's office in Regina, Saskatchewan. Larry, his friend from university who had joined Continental with him, was already there with his wife. Self had been best man at their wedding, in England. Lisa was planning to open a boutique in the city centre. He helped them now setting up the shop and they offered him an interest in the business. Glad to have a diversion from his work in the engineering herd, he leapt at the opportunity.

Acorn was a new fashion boutique. Lisa's family had connections with the rag trade in London. She selected miniskirts and hot pants from wholesalers' catalogues and they were air-freighted to her.

Self found a vacant store they could lease in a new shopping centre, where passing shoppers could be lured in to buy trendy gear. He also designed, constructed and decorated the shop interior, installing lighting and the front window display. Adjacent storeowners, who had employed professional companies to install their shops, complained to the building management that Acorn's DIY shop fit was not allowed. The trio had to employ tradespeople to take down their installations and reinstall them, copying from their design.

Once they had established Acorn, it was a great success. Lisa sold London Carnaby Street fashions to farmers' wives and daughters, with a huge mark up. Their brands were trendy and buyers beat a path to their door. There wasn't much for Self to do as a co-owner of the shop.

When a garment wouldn't sell, Lisa would display it in the store window, at a price three times higher than the purchase cost, labelling it 'SALE 30%'. It usually sold quickly. Self imagined buyers as herd animals, who assumed the most valuable garments would be prominently displayed, highly priced and heavily discounted.

They considered developing a chain of shops across Canada. Their experience with Acorn had left them with no illusions: retailing was a desert. Starting a fashion empire would be demanding and uncertain. It would be an accomplishment others could admire, but they didn't care about that. Keeping it running would be too tedious.

Self had enjoyed working in a team with Lisa and Larry. The money wasn't enough for he or Larry to want to leave their professional jobs with Continental, where they could expect promotion to well paid positions soon. Self didn't have the sense of fashion needed to open his own store, or to anticipate shopper tastes. Nor did he have employer skills to hire a shop manager.

When Larry was transferred to Toronto, they sold Acorn as an operating business. A year later when Self visited the new owners, they said custom had fallen away. Whereas Lisa had bought latest fashions from London, the new owners were buying locally and less fashionably. The store needed a fashion makeover and new suppliers.

Self continued with the herd in his engineering job, enjoying the work now. The boutique business had been lucrative, but hard work was required and good luck. He preferred to focus his effort on serving the corporate herd and gaining an eminent position within it.

It was likely that in Regina, a small city, Self's double-timing would be noticed by Continental's herd masters, but no-one complained to him. His orientation assignment in Regina finished and he was transferred to distant Calgary. His involvement with Acorn boutique ended, except for banking a fat cheque, when they sold it.

He had gained business experience and he used it to lift his service to the engineering herd to the next level.

PART 3
CAMEL

Self worked hard in Calgary, with senior engineers keeping him on a tight rein.

He clung to his goal: to stop the Cold War. He became interested in economics and politics. His task was large and he began to consider how he wanted the UK to be governed. He wanted people's views represented in a democracy but he had no interest in politics. But rather than them seeking individual freedom as a libertarian, he wanted communal control for the greatest good of the greatest number.

Self doubted that egalitarianism would result in a centralised state directed by a political elite. On the other hand, he wanted World government to end the Cold War and bring peace. He needed to find out about socialism but it was frowned on at Continental Oil. He asked university students at his rugby club about socialism, but that popular candidates in the student council elections were frequently socialists.

It took Self several years at Continental Oil to achieve a camel role, as in Nietzsche's allegory. He was strong in spirit and underwent a spiritual journey to self-actualisation. Unlike the others in the herd he had come from, he was happy to kneel and take on the heaviest burdens. His spirit gradually assumed a 'camel' role, a slave relied on to carry heavy burdens, dominated, humiliated, with unrequited affection for those he served. It was a lonely role and Self feared being inconsequential.

He was seconded to Continental's engineering headquarters, to work in a camel role. The work was mundane, sometimes arduous and prolonged. Although he understood what to do, he had no assistance and could never dominate, never tell others what to do, even if he knew what had to be done and they wanted to know.

He worked exceedingly hard towards getting a personal domain, avoiding taking unnecessary risks. His striving brought him happiness, rejoicing in his strength. His camel role was valued in the workplace. His recognition brought him only momentary pleasure because his attention was on his domain and external control he could possess.

CHAPTER 12
SLAVES

Self worked in an office building in downtown Calgary. Conditions were comfortable, with heated underground car parking and he was not outside in cold winter weather or summer heat, except at weekends, when he would go skiing or camping. He drove to the Rocky Mountains with friends from work and unwound from the stresses of the office.

Self wanted employment that was interesting and responsible and engineers competed fiercely, but covertly, to be assigned to exciting projects that would lever them up the hierarchy. Young professional engineers were salaried, but virtually indentured, receiving unfairly low salaries, like being in an apprenticeship. The rationale was that their abasement would later be rewarded by promotion and managerial privileges: high pay; a secretary; assistants; innovative projects; external assignments; kudos; overseas travel; an expense account; tickets to games; and a company car. They could get company-arranged mortgages at low interest, although they could have to stay in those jobs to repay the loans. Changing companies was frowned on, as if engineers were property of their employer, like slaves.

The best assignments were hard to get. Opportunities were not widely known and ambitious engineers touted their curriculum vitae to managers who could inform them of openings and influence their selection.

There was a bandwagon, or Matthew, Effect. The Bible says:

'For whosoever hath, to him shall be given, and he shall have more abundance: but whosoever hath not, from him shall be taken away even that he hath.' Matt 13:12.

When opinion leaders holding powerful positions favoured an opening, there was an avalanche of applications for it from their followers. Early birds had an advantage and newcomers like Self usually applied too late to be considered. There were a few positions having unattractive features that no-one applied for, as if there could be a stigma from applying for them.

He spent his days at his desk transposing oilfield performance data, interpreting it and suggesting to his supervisor downhole oil well workovers that could increase production. He was able to predict when a steam injection cycle, to melt the tar so it could be pumped out, had been completed. It felt good to him to be managing an oilfield and contributing to practical results.

Self knew that to gain more responsibility he would have to differentiate himself. He traded on his high intelligence and ability to identify the best opportunities. When mischief-makers started rumours and lemming-like rushes occurred, Self was not taken in. His insight was that the majority of workers were virtual slaves, without choice of activity, performing within the norms of the culture, for not much recompense.

Engineers were conditioned to describe how the world worked, rather than to consider philosophical aspects, debate, or discuss the meaning of what they were doing. Their work had little intellectual challenge and the jokes and gossip did not sufficiently stimulate Self's imagination.

He was assigned to an oil field northeast of Edmonton to implement technological changes he had worked on in the office. For several months, he lived at the Cold Lake township in a trailer with two technicians. Nearby was the Cold Lake Air Base of the Royal Canadian Airforce, with 10,000 personnel whose work enabled about 10 pilots yearly, to learn to fly F101 fighters.

Self joined the Base's flying club, went to ground school and took flying lessons. They boasted aerobatic planes flown by stoned-out members, who got lost in three dimensions. He had some hair-raising experiences. Within about six months he passed the test for a private pilot's licence.

When he returned to Edmonton, he continued flying at the Edmonton Flying Club. He flew solo across country but when he could not locate features in the whited-out countryside, he became lost, almost running out of fuel and deciding to turn back. He had been at 12,000 feet going west and climbed up to an odd number of thousands of feet and headed east at 13,000 feet, as he had practiced. As he climbed higher, he could see a familiar lake on the horizon and knew where he was.

He practiced flying doing circuits at the Edmonton Industrial Airport. It was always busy, with fifteen, or more, light planes in the circuit, doing touch and go landings. When a passenger jet wanted to land, the small planes had to make way for the jet to come in on final leg and land.

One day, Self had finished his practice and was on the main runway heading for the flying club, when the control tower called.

'EFD237 attention. Clear main runway. Jet aircraft on final.'

Self didn't know which taxiway would lead to the flying club, because there had been a change of runway while he was in the air and he was disoriented. He didn't know whether to go left or right at the next intersection, because he didn't recognise the flying club hangar. Going the wrong way could take a long taxi to correct. He dithered on the main runway.

'EFD237 clear main runway immediately.'

Moments later, there was a roar and a passenger jet went over, a few metres up, the wash throwing his plane about. It climbed away to go around for another attempt.

The control tower abused him on air, for a near accident. He inferred his direction finding skills were lacking. It shook him and he never piloted again. Pilots have to anticipate difficulties and react quickly. Self had always found the safety checks and navigation precautions tedious, perhaps because he had no burning desire to keep passengers safe and happy. He preferred to relax in the cockpit. He decided to quit piloting before he had an accident.

He wanted recognition at work. He thought he could become a manager and applied to sit the company's management aptitude test, by completing a questionnaire, at his desk. The questions were multi-choice and some were puzzling. He was asked 'Which would you prefer, to work as a truck driver, or as a ballet dancer?' Another was: 'Did you ever want to have sex with your mother?'

Puzzled by the relevance of the questions, Self sought explanation from the psychologist administering the test.

'How will they decide which answers indicate management aptitude?' he asked.

'There are no right answers', the psychologist said. 'We pick out oddballs. If your answers are similar to the others', you are suitable. If yours are weird, management is not for you.'

'It seems to me a travesty that Continental's managers are selected to be ordinary,' Self objected. 'As leaders, they should be extraordinary.'

'A good manager has to be able to anticipate underlings,' the psychologist said.

'Aren't underlings answers merely sycophantic?' Self asked.

'Empathy with others is wanted.'

'In a stable environment, empathy with underlings could be a prescription for paternalism,' Self said. 'Our environment is changing, with new tasks, development and innovation. Managers need to have creative leadership abilities.'

'Sorry, we don't test for those.'

When Self was not selected, it confirmed management's conservatism and his oddball status. He was a loner and his peers' attitudes were quite unknown to him. He realised that he needed more experience in the herd.

He was advised by a manager friend to lead other workers by expediting their work, informally as an engineering counsellor, adviser and strategist. He could demonstrate his intelligence and nous, by service to the others, rather than by taking a psychological test. He could be a coordinator, enabling co-operation, a leader without responsibility for operations.

Self attended to the day to day running of the department, like an administration clerk. He was recognised for serving others as a 'camel', doing the heavy lifting, suffering tedium, receiving a modest salary. It was step up from the herd, but still feudal, with obligation to a superior day-to-day. His position could be a stepping stone into management, when he would receive a high salary. His spirit was ascending and his resistance freed him from slavery in the herd, determined to fulfil his camel spirit, his distinction being obedience.

CHAPTER 13
OFFICE RIVALRY

Self's striving became more like a camel and less like a slave. His behaviour was scrutinized and tested to determine his position in the informal pecking order, where advancement was publicly recognised.

His work group, a team of about 20 engineers, gathered every morning in an informal circle around the group manager, sipping from cups of hot beverages. It was a social ritual. People could join the circle anywhere, but the more senior members stood near the manager and newcomers stood on the opposite side. The manager would start a discussion about a topic in the news, such as the score in a ball game. Others gave their views, such as consequences, controversy, or joked with humorous word play. One person spoke at a time with everyone looking at the speaker. Anything unusual could be turned against the speaker, causing his embarrassment. Self quickly learned not to give unusual views or opinions and said little. After 20 minutes the gathering dispersed as people returned to their desks.

The purpose seemed to be to establish the pre-eminence of the manager, senior staff and their favourites, who could rule on and face down the ideas of those lower in the hierarchy. Senior sages gave their 'gut feelings' as if age made intuition respectable. New staff learned that if they spoke, they could expect to have their ideas challenged and overruled. Senior staff would challenge junior staff but seldom vice versa. In this way the pecking order was renewed and maintained.

The manager asked Self what type of car he owned.
'A Jaguar Mark 7.'

'Interesting. It is a vintage car, designed for English weather. How are you getting on with it?'

'Not well.'

He told them about the problems, starting the engine with temperatures of minus forty, brittle hood hinge castings and door handles that snapped.

They picked holes in the old foreign technology and recommended technologies that better complied with the Canadian climate. It was predictable and normative control of individual behaviour, by gaslighting or bullying. Continental's seniors regarded their role as keeping the herd together. Self disliked the social manipulation of these supposedly 'social' rituals. He wanted to get to know people, but interaction was stilted and tense.

Other meetings considered results from field operations, actions required and matters to be investigated. Unexpected events, such as low productivity or accidents would be reported by the responsible engineers and the group would mull over responses needed. These forums were the beating heart of engineering, with some posturing and bullying. He gained experience, his participation increased and he became a trusted voice.

Mistakes occurred because the oil production technology was new and the geology was only partly known. The forums sought solutions to problems and avoided laying blame vindictively. It was recognised that progress involved taking risks. Self was sometimes frustrated that when there were risks, senior engineers held sway with unreasonable caution. Daring was lacking.

The group had a custom of sending each of them in turn to the horse racetrack with a dollar from each of them collected weekly, plus last week's winnings. At the end of the year, any money remaining would be spent on a party. It was an opportunity to benefit the group by skill. Self never gambled and had no skill at betting but he imagined he could use his experience of Rocket to pick a winning horse.

When it was his turn, the kitty had $40 from last time plus $25 collected that week. Enlarging the kitty conferred prestige on the proponent and conversely losing from it brought shame. Self dutifully inspected the prospective racehorses in the saddling enclosure and bet on the ones he thought would win. After 4 of the 5 races scheduled, he had no winners at all and had lost all the kitty money. To avoid returning empty-handed, he bet $40 from his personal money on the final race. If he won, he would not divulge that he had used his own money and recover the kudos he had lost with the kitty money.

The horses leapt out of the starting gate, all except the one he had bet on, which sauntered out sedately. It stayed at the back of the field until the last lap, when it sprinted into the lead. It was an outsider, the odds were long and Self imagined returning with a substantial sum, even enlarging the kitty. But on the home bend, it was leading by a hundred metres when it stumbled, fell and couldn't get up. Stewards surrounded it with screens and a shot was heard.

When he told it at the office, heads wagged and they were too polite to accuse him of being a Jonah or jinxing the horse. The social penalty concerned him less than did the destruction of the horse. His acumen as a punter was also destroyed. He never went to a racetrack again.

Other social mores were that no-one worked after hours. When Self stayed at the office to finish tasks, or took work home, it was frowned upon by other engineers.

'Working outside hours reduces others' working conditions,' they told him. 'They have obligations to their families.'

Self regarded these admonitions as intrusive overreach and slavish. He ignored them when he could.

The same zealots expected him to wear a suit, white shirt, tie and shoes at work. Self interpreted it as a tradition of conformance to a corporate ideal. The clothes worn were not practical garb, nor even comfortable. However, Self conformed without qualms, anything to avoid a fashion parade.

Achievement was rewarded with privileges. Lack of conformity was punished by taking away privileges. When Self started at Continental, his working space was a bare cubicle in an open plan office area, surrounded by moveable unadorned screens. When a supervisor wanted to reward him, paintings were hung on his walls, a carpet was laid on his floor, his area was expanded, a chair and table for his visitors provided and a potted plant put on his desk.

In a neighbouring cubicle was an engineer who had offended management. They wanted him to leave. His privileges were removed and the walls of his office moved in until he couldn't reach his desk. He soon quit.

Self found the office culture stultifying and oppressive. He focussed on moving up the hierarchy to a more rewarding position. If he could distinguish himself from his peers, as a 'camel', his diligence could gain promotion to a position in management.

CHAPTER 14
SPRING BREAK UP

Self tried to raise his status, among engineers at his workplace, by doing difficult tasks diligently and responsibly. He performed services people wanted, adopting a camel spirit. His helping of others and his social skills made him prominent at work, attracting supporters and detractors jealous of his influence. He sought agency, acting for others in contexts and relationships that brought him closer to self-mastery.

John was a friend, a rookie engineer who had been in the same cohort when Self started at Continental. He was gentle, kind and sincere. He was in a different section, where he had a similar 'camel' role. They shared an apartment in Edmonton.

John invited Self to go with him to a Spring Break Up party, at his parents' place in the Rocky Mountains near Banff. John's family looked after horses used for tourist rides in the summer. The horses wintered on the mountain, snowed in at their stables.

'Spring break up is when the roads become driveable,' said John. 'Neighbours have been cut-off from each other for months by deep snow and look forward to a party. People have been practicing their music and want to play, sing and dance together.'

Self had packed his thermals and guitar. They drove about 300 miles into the Rockies, along roads cleared by snowploughs. As they negotiated the ravines and pine forests, John drove gingerly with studded car tyres along the icy roads. They went in as far as they could reach, between towering pines laden with snow. There were slithering crashes, as snow fell from branches.

John's father was waiting with a rubber-tracked vehicle, fitted with a dozer blade to clear its path. They rode inside as it clawed its way up the mountainside, pushing through to the house. The road was slushy, with melt water running away in rivulets, becoming torrents. They arrived at a perfect log cabin on a hilltop, in a clearing in the pine forest. There was smoke curling from the chimney. Inside was a large room, with screens and beds pushed back.

Self met John's mother and his sister Susan, about his own age. She was pretty with a country drawl, breathless and excited. She had been holed up there all winter. She was lively, getting ready to play her banjo for the dance. She and self were soon making music together. The whole family were musical and had spent the winter fiddling, strumming, plucking, yodelling and carrying on like hillbillies.

John's mum was a perfect cowgirl, with a frayed suede leather skirt and a 5 gallon hat.

His father's legs were bowed, wide enough for a horse to go between.

The phone network hadn't reached them yet and they hadn't talked to anyone for about six months. Their nearest neighbour was several kilometres away, but the snow was deep and they may as well have been on the Moon. John and his mother set to cooking up eggs, bacon and beans. Self washed them down with the best coffee he had ever tasted.

That evening, the neighbours arrived, delighted to renew old acquaintance. The cabin exploded into life, with Self and Susan bashing out Beatles songs and everyone dancing. The room was a riot of gyrating bodies with people leaping about wildly. Susan's banjo and singing outshone Self's guitar playing. Without printed music, he couldn't remember the chord sequences, but faked the melody and kept the rhythm going. The dancers didn't seem to mind and after a while Susan called a halt, for a break.

Self was under Susan's spell. She was a lovely girl and he was entranced. They did House in New Orleans, with Susan playing fiddle. Then they played You Ain't Nothing but a Hound Dog, Hey Jude, Johnny Cash, Joan Baez, Kris Kristofferson, Me and Bobby McGhee and Dolly Parton's Coat of Many Colours.

He leaned his guitar in a corner and went outside for a smoke. When he came back, his guitar strings had been slashed with a knife.

The blade had cut into the guitar neck viciously. It seemed like malice and Self wondered whom he had angered. Susan seemed disconcerted, as if she might know of someone who could have done it. John thought it was one of the boys chasing his sister. But he didn't say which one. Susan was shaken, but continued with banjo solos.

People who lived there were tuned to basic civilities and maintaining friendships, but there was a guy giving Self the evil eye, who seemed to be chasing Susan. There could be enmity towards city people like Self, using their homelands as a playground. The attack on his guitar could be from jealousy, an attempt to break up his music gig with Susan, rather than from personal enmity. Anyway, it was successful, for it stopped Self from playing his guitar.

Self could have been seen as a lion, because his music was dominant and because Susan was with him. An aggressive individual having a dragon spirit could have interpreted Self's interest in Susan as making a play for her. Self would not fight Evil Eye. Retribution would have been pointless.

Self realised that John's family's care for horses and tourists was humble servitude, not unlike the horses' slavery. Between family members and their horses there was respectful reciprocity. Horses have a special place in humans' history, kept on farms before tractors and replaced in cavalry by tanks. Self admired horses' stalwart service, with only camels coming close as slaves. His 'camel' role among engineers at Continental usually preoccupied his thoughts, but seemed far away up here.

Next day, he waded through the snow outside in the forest clearing. The sun was bright, the air clean, with the branches dropping snow and dripping. Underfoot there was water gurgling into streams.

Whatever the motive for the attack on his guitar, it didn't separate him from Susan. They stayed all day and went back to the city on Sunday evening. He said goodbye to Susan and went back to work on Monday with John.

He remained friends with John and Susan and took her out a couple of times when she came into Calgary. She was a lovely girl. He had met country girls in England but they were demure whereas Susan was all fun and laughter. Self had sensed she was not really his type, too dependent. She gave him her banjo mandolin. He never learned to play it, regrettably. He met up with her again in Calgary but neither of them seemed to want a relationship. His plans did not include having a partner for many years. He would not start a relationship in which she could be hurt, because she seemed vulnerable and his plans were too uncertain. On life's trail, it's easy to take a wrong turn and he knew he could never go back.

His friendship with John continued and they often helped each other with their jobs. The engineering section relied on Self to administer computing services. Because the technology was changing, it was demanding work. His service was appreciated because he was skilled, thorough and not discouraged by opposition or detractors.

Chapter 15
Computer Models

Self had a 'camel' role in coordinating development of computer models for Continental's Canadian oilfields. They were numerical models that tried out solutions to meet the conditions specified by the engineers. The models were used to predict oil production, to find if a flow rate was declining and where to bore new wells. Self's job was to coordinate between the engineers and the production people who used the predictions. He nominated engineers with the best experience to develop each model. When a model was modified, he made sure the change had been tested and sent it to those who had asked for it, in time to meet their schedule. He billed the engineers' hours to each project, on their behalf.

Self's role was a clerk rather than a manager. He was like a camel, who carried reports, reliably and promptly. He optimised workflow and team members valued his coordination.

'When constructing a model, it's easy to forget what it has to do,' an engineer said. 'We are on the inside, but we have to please people on the outside.'

'Self helps us with that,' another engineer said. 'He makes the most of what we do.'

Self loved his work. He was reliable and strong. Continental Oil sent him for training to their research department in Houston, Texas. After training, his task was to evaluate a numerical model of a Canadian oilfield, developed by their engineers, who trusted him to trial it.

Before he could run the model, he had to prepare a box of punched cards, with data input changes and system commands. He submitted it to operators who ran a Central Processing Unit, enclosed in an air conditioned room that took up the ground floor area of the research centre. It was operated from magnetic tape storage and had banks of tape drivers.

There were two IBM 360 units linked together, reputed to be the most powerful computers in the world at that time. After submitting his cards, he waited, doing other work, to receive the output 24 hours later. If it had run okay, it would be a pile of paper, with production predictions, day after day, going 20 years into the future. Sometimes there was a message: 'Input error. Run failed.' Alternatively it might be: 'Calculation terminated; no convergence.' Or: 'Output print format error. Job unable to be completed.' He waited for a block of printout with the message 'Run completed.' Progress was slow without today's desktop computers. Now a model can be coded and run by one person working at a desktop screen, where several had been needed.

The overall objective was simulating reservoir performance by computation. There were two modelling processes. Most effort went into classical simulation, which represented flows of heat, oil, water and gas in the reservoir rock, using equations verified by others' laboratory experiments. Effects such as flow to the well bore would be calculated from a change in modelled conditions, such as a new bore with a pump to extract oil. Production quantities would be predicted by iterative calculation, repeating until a credible prediction had been obtained.

The other type of model used a 'black-box' approach that simply extrapolated oilfield production data. It had no theory of flow and deduced outcomes assuming current performance would continue. This worked best in the short term but was unreliable when the oilfield was nearing depletion.

Self enjoyed the work because it combined technical challenge with human interaction. He spent his time getting the model to run past hang ups. Predictions had to go forward many years, without hanging due to calculation problems. Persistent shortfalls could require engineers to recode parts of the model. His job was to adjust the model input settings to obtain confident predictions.

He wrote reports that held the team together, identifying responsibilities. He had personal goals of rising in the organisation, with a will to succeed. He was slowly gaining control of his own destiny.

Self was strong in spirit, as a camel undergoing a spiritual journey to self-actualisation. The camel was a carrier, a herd animal, happy to kneel down and take on the burdens of his role. Self rejoiced in his strength. There was pleasure in doing work that supported so many people, but because there was no visible output, few knew what he was doing and sometimes he was lonely.

He was conscientious and when the models were inaccurate, he was critical of them. His opinions were not always accepted by the modellers, because he was young and inexperienced.

Once, when his reports indicated that the engineering herd was about to fall over a credibility cliff, unless predictions improved, it made him unpopular. Self lacked academic credentials and was overruled. The researchers all had PhDs or masters' degrees. Debates were abstract, couched in mathematical logic. He wanted to acquire qualifications with which he could hold his own. He planned to travel in South America and then to go back to university in the UK to do a PhD.

Self slowly gained practical experience and his advice became respected. He was no longer subjected to humiliating domination and his slavery was replaced by serfdom. It was a feudal relationship, in which although he had limited control over implementation of the technology, he was under management's protection. He resented his dependence on them.

Continental management in Houston sent him back to Canada, presumably because he had shot himself in the foot with his negative evaluation of the models. He was given other work to do. It was not an outcome he wanted and interrupted his service as a camel, in which role he had differentiated himself from the herd. He had no prospect of a management position and decided to quit.

'I want authority,' he thought. 'If I had a PhD, they would listen to me.'

He applied for UK government for research money for three years to do a PhD and they awarded him a grant, because he had achieved a first class honours undergraduate degree.

'First I want to do some travelling.'
He resigned, saying he would return and apply for a job in four years' time.

CHAPTER 16
BRICK DELIVERY

After quitting Continental, Self drove his Rambler station wagon across Canada and down through the USA. He was up for adventure and joined hippies migrating to Canada and California, to protest the war in Vietnam. He went on to Central America and South America. His holiday lasted a year, during which he recovered from the three years of servitude he had spent in the corporate herd. He wanted to do PhD research in the UK, that would enable him to command his own territory, with the spirit and freedom of a lion.

He began by forsaking his short hair, tie and suit. He acquired a Fu Manchu moustache, beard, long hair, poncho and love beads. He picked up hitch hikers, smoked their grass and learned the hippy culture as he drove south, sleeping in the back of his vehicle.

He was in Mexico for several months. The joy of traveling alone, in his own vehicle, was that he could choose where he went, when to go and who to go with. Sometimes, for a change, he stayed at inexpensive hotels. He was in control of his life and his confidence in his own domain grew in his interaction with others.

In Mexico, he spent a couple of weeks seeing Mexico City, then headed for Acapulco. With him were an Australian couple, both actors. From them he learned how to attract attention in public, with disdain for the herd. Parading their gear, they attracted audiences, gave frequent peace signs and laughed a lot.

When they reached the Pacific coast, they slept in hammocks on a beach for two weeks and body surfed. Together they bought several kilogram bricks of Acapulco Gold, potent marijuana grown locally. They followed a guide along a footpath up a hill, between poor adobe houses with starving donkeys, to a wizened supplier. They sampled a joint and it was amazing high quality. They paid the asking price and were pleased with their purchase.

They smoked, talked, slept and surfed in rotation. It was blissful. Self stayed high for days. He was so spaced out, when waves tumbled him under, he had difficulty finding the surface and was lucky not to drown.

He drove the Australians around subserviently, stoned, with camel obedience.

'Why are you driving so slowly?' the actor asked him.

'I didn't know I was,' he replied, surfacing from a daydream.

'Look,' the other said, opening the car door, revealing the roadside. It was passing by at a snail's pace. He had been too stoned to notice.

'I'll speed up,' he said.

They met an American hippy with a camper van. He proceeded to undo panels and stash grass in floor cavities.

'I'll take this back to the States,' he said. 'The FBI are looking for me and I have to be careful. I got caught once.'

He departed for the USA with his cargo. A few days later there was a newspaper story with a picture of his burned out vehicle by the highway. A body had been found beside it. Self felt vulnerable because he had a brick stored under his own dashboard, among the wires. The stench suffused his vehicle, smelling like lawn clippings. It was a giveaway if police investigated.

He wasn't concerned. A person's response to danger is decided in a marble-sized part of their brain, the amygdala, under the back of the head. In adolescents and young adult males, it responds weakly to danger, but with age it puts out adrenalin to freeze, fight or flight. After age 30 males are better at applying these strategies than they are in their 20s.

He was 24 and barely registered any peril as he drove across Mexico, through Yucutan and down through the jungle into Belize. He was aware his stash could be penalized at the border, but the risk seemed low and it was not a capital offence, as it was in some countries. He did not fear the FBI, nor did he consider what the British government's response would be if he was caught. He continued because he was an adventurer, seeking kudos from other hippies.

Much to his relief, the border guards let him into British Honduras without a search. In Belize City he met some locals returned from New York, wanting drugs to take back. They carried flick knives, threatened him and discovered his kilo. He gave it to them willingly, glad to see the back of it, because it was compromising his safety. His amygdala was active at last and he realised he had been lucky.

Self's station wagon developed a fault. A local person advised him to take it to The Mennonites, a Christian sect, living as a colony in the hinterland.

'They are the best car mechanics in the country,' his informant stated, 'but they don't drive cars.'

Puzzled he went to their colony, an agricultural community in an enclave that technology had passed by. The olde-worlde workshop was equipped with home-made tools, without electricity.

'We don't drive cars. For us community is everything,' the mechanic told him. 'We reject cars for personal use – not because they're bad for the environment, but because travel by horse and cart stop settlements growing too far apart. We believe motorised vehicles are inherently bad – we use tractors for farming – but rather the emphasis is on the importance of community. We use horses for transport. If we had access to a car, we could be tempted to leave, but the limited travel range of horses and carts keeps Mennonite settlements close-knit.

'It's the same with most technologies, we consider what they would do to our community and limit those we will accept. We strive for self-sufficiency, mutual aid and peace. It is often assumed that we fear the all-consuming nature of technology, but our choice has more to do with scepticism and adherence to principle.'

As they talked, a horse-drawn buggy wheeled by, with a man in a tall top hat and a woman in a smock dress.

The mechanic interrupted.

'Can I have a look at that newspaper?'

He pointed to a newspaper on the floor of the station wagon. Self handed it to him.

'I haven't seen a newspaper for years.'

While his car was being fixed, Self talked with the mechanic.

'What do our modern economies look like to sect members?'

'We don't want to live in one,' he said.

'Do you prefer the capitalist or socialist countries?'

'Centrally planned economies, whether socialist or capitalist, are virtually the same,' he said, as he raised his vehicle on a car jack.

'Both systems have a central authority directing economic activities, resources allocation, prices and societal objectives. But in centrally planned economies the state eliminates private ownership to ensure collective benefit. Socialism eliminates class distinctions whereas capitalism's focus is on motivation by profit and market forces. Socialism can suffer from bureaucracy whereas capitalism has challenges of inequality affecting social welfare.'

Self was amazed at his lucidity. It seemed that he actively discussed these points as articles of the Mennonite faith.

'There are similarities,' Self agreed. 'But there are major differences with socialists in individual roles and relativities.'

'We Mennonites are collectivists and attuned to the egalitarianism of socialism, but not to being governed. We value individual freedom.'

'Your self-sufficiency is closer to capitalism than socialism, don't you think?' Self said.

'We reject much of the technology of capitalism.'

'Is control of technology worth it, to get self-sufficiency?' asked Self.

'Yes, because our independence means everything to us,' the mechanic said. 'The technologies destabilize us.'

'Technology brings change.'

'Change is not always good. The Luddites wanted to stabilize employment in the cotton industry in England, but 17 were hanged in 1816 and others were exiled to Australia,

'If technologies could be restricted by mandate,' said Self, 'there would be a long queue of candidates for banning and others for exemption. My ideal economy would have freedom of use of technology.'

'Freedoms of technology, of property ownership and of government all have to be decided,' he said. 'You would be in the hands of lawyers, who have their own technologies. Our communities would be destroyed.'

The mechanic finished and Self paid him a modest sum. He kept the newspaper.

Self wanted to become a PhD student of national planning in England when he returned. The attraction was to do work that could make a difference. He would be a person of consequence, unlike his role at Continental Oil, where he had been a slave of the corporation. He had quit his job to maintain self-respect. He had gained self-respect and no longer would he be a camel. He would be a lion.

PART 4
LION

Self's spirit yearned to transform from the subservience of a camel to the dominion of a lion. His ambition was to be able to do whatever he wanted, using any legal means to conquer opponents, taking control of his own destiny, becoming lord of the desert. He wanted control over the austere arena in which the superpowers were engaged in the Cold War, with ICBM threats, posturing at the Berlin Wall and fighting in Vietnam.

The Cold War was characterized by ideological competition between the two superpowers. The United States, as a capitalist and democratic country, promoted the idea of free-market capitalism, individual freedoms, and democracy. On the other hand, the Soviet Union, as a socialist state, advocated for the principles of communism, emphasizing state ownership of the means of production and the goal of creating a classless society.

The Cold War saw a massive arms race between the U.S. and the Soviet Union. Both superpowers engaged in the development of nuclear weapons and military technologies, leading to an unprecedented level of global military spending. This competition was driven by ideological differences, with both sides seeking to demonstrate the superiority of their respective system.

Self was intrigued by the antipathy between the ideologies of capitalism and communism, wondering if the conflict between them was reconcilable, with potential for a rapprochement. His PhD could seek compromise between capitalist and socialist governments for their different variables of national economic planning.

He aimed first to discover how his lion spirit could fence-sit the Cold War impasse, in a politically, economically and philosophically sound position. He would spend a year in Central and South America, experiencing new places, political conditions and alternative lifestyles, before he would commit to devising a solution for World peace. Despite some fatalism on both sides, many people wanted a fair resolution, without a fight.

He planned to carve ideas for a solution to the Cold War, from the raw clay of national planning in the countries he would visit, making him famous. His spirit was egotistical as befitted a lion, because his mission was solitary and there was no-one else he could impress.

He wanted to understand national planning in the socialist countries he visited and if he could, compromise socialism with capitalism.

CHAPTER 17
GALAPAGOS

After Belize, he drove on through Central America to Panama, where he sold his station wagon, gained freedom from car hassles, used public transport and avoided being extorted at national borders. He flew to Bogota and bussed to Quito in Ecuador. He bought a ticket on the Ecuadorean Navy's patrol boat departing from Guayaquil, for a visit to the Galapagos Islands, at the Equator in the South Pacific. There were about 50 passengers, with separate quarters for men and women, in holds with single hammocks.

When they crossed the Equator, crew and passengers paid homage to King Neptune, Ruler of the Deep. Those aboard who were crossing the line for the first time were tried in his court and sentenced to terrible privations. They were required to quaff a mixture of diesel oil and urine, then crawl under a net sluiced by a fire hose. It was done in fun, with such enthusiasm that some crew members became ill. Initiation of the passengers was kinder.

Self felt privileged to be there. He was excited to be going to the place where Charles Darwin formulated his theory of natural selection, important to Self's understanding of how the natural world functioned. The book Origin of the Species was published in 1859, deposing God and religion, with continuing controversy. Nietzsche declared 23 years later, in his book 'The Gay Science': 'God remains dead. And we have killed him.' Self's visit to the place of Darwin's discovery empowered him to reject God but his scepticism wouldn't let him dismiss the possibility of a God and like Darwin he proclaimed himself agnostic.

Self had never believed there was a God, but until he realised the theory of evolution, he didn't have any other explanation for the existence of the natural world than religion, morality, history and tradition. He now had evidence that contradicted these systems of belief and he consigned them, as Nietzsche had done, to the dustbin.

He was intrigued why Darwin had studied the remote Galapagos environment. The islands were quite recent in origin, emerging from beneath the ocean during the last one to five million years by volcanism, with hot spots in the mantle bursting through overlying tectonic plates in the ocean floor, creating sterile islands. They had been populated since by living things that had drifted there by sea, or been carried by birds and animals, or brought by humans in boats from the mainland. Or they could have evolved there.

Nietzsche despised Darwin's theory. He believed that animals stumble through life unaware of what they are doing or why they are doing it. Self speculated that if Nietzsche had gone to the Galapagos too and seen evidence of ancestral types, he would have credited natural environments with determinism and animals with learning of behaviour that enabled their survival. Darwin's view was that will-to-power was less important for human survival than Nietzsche believed. Nietzsche had spent most of his thought energy considering the interior of humans, mainly the brain. His rejection of evolution theory was probably more neglect than antithesis. Recent theories of the evolution of the brain would probably have interested him and he would have accepted Darwin's theory.

Self could touch wild birds and animals, because they had no fear of him. On the islands, human predation had been limited by isolation. Darwin was able to closely observe beaks and other adaptations of finches in meticulous detail and he developed credible theories of how their evolution had responded to natural environments.

He saw how large-billed finches could feed more efficiently on large, hard seeds, whereas smaller billed finches fed on small, soft seeds. When small, soft seeds became rare, large-billed finches survived better and there were more larger-billed birds in the following generation. When large, hard seeds became rare, the opposite occurred. It was inference, but reasonable.

Self couldn't fault Darwin's reasoning, but he knew his belief in evolution was a different type of faith than his own faith in regular science, which could be tested by experiments in laboratories, whereas evolution could not. Like a leaky boat afloat on a sea of faith in science, evolution wasn't quite water tight. Darwin had explained how useful variations were transferred by selection to the succeeding generation, when the fittest survived. It was a plausible process, but couldn't be observed, only inferred.

Lamarck's competing idea was that transfer of all acquired traits would have been too slow for the variations in bill types to have emerged in the brief time available. He theorised that organisms altered their behaviour in response to environmental change. Their changed behaviour, in turn, modified their organs, and their offspring inherited those 'improved' structures. It would require processes of inheritance of structures to be boosted by striving to be faster than selection by the environment. Lamarck's theory had been revived as epigenetics. This theory had inference too and Self had to be content with the ambiguity.

Self wanted to discern evolution in its many different appearances. Evolution was the cornerstone of his understanding of the natural world and mankind's effects. Whether evolution was driven by creation, mutation, or by the wilful drive of aberrant types, he could not tell, but it didn't matter. Darwin's processes of descent, gradualism and natural selection were disputable, but they explained the evidence of inheritance. But these processes were slower than the will-to-power with which a lion contested its domain.

Like Nietzsche, Self was emboldened by Darwin's theory to adopt a posture of personal primacy, as if the survival of his kind depended on him in his domain. When he had quit Continental Oil his ego was flaccid, but on the road his spirit had grown leonine, searching for a domain to rule over.

Self's will-to-power operated within the ecology of his domain. The importance of domain in heredity had been underlined by Che Guevara, on the path to becoming a Marxist revolutionary, twenty years earlier during his coming-of-age motor cycle adventure through five South American countries. The medical student's travels made him more conscious of a common South American civilization and awoke in him a pan-American vision.

'The division of America into unstable and illusionary nations is completely fictional, we constitute a single mestizo race, which from Mexico to the Magellan straits bears notable ethnographical similarities,'

'And so, in an attempt to rid myself of the weight of small-minded provincialism, I propose a toast to Peru and to a United Latin America.'

Like Che Guevara, Self wanted to rule over the lonely desert, to become lord of the desert, to capture his own meaning and freedom to fulfil his destiny. He would rule over a natural order, either evolving by Darwin's theory of natural selection, or being changed by artificial selection. He wanted to see in the Galapagos a natural state of nature and hoped humans had conserved it.

He patted the shell of one of the few remaining Giant Tortoises. They had been plundered and stacked alive in ships' holds, to replenish the stores with fresh meat. Until tourism developed, the Islands had few visitors. Besides tortoises, visitors had probably caught birds, iguanas, fish and seals, but the numbers taken were small and the ecology remained pristine. Rats had come with humans and simply invaded. Some feral species had been brought to the Islands for agricultural and aesthetic purposes. Pigs, goats and chickens provided food. Cats and dogs were brought for companionship. Ornamental plants were introduced to create gardens and had escaped, causing problems. Human damage to the ecology was significant.

Self was pleased to find that in most places in the Galapagos, wild animals did not hide from humans as they did on the mainland. He supposed that on both sides of the iron curtain, 1,381 kilometres long, between the German Democratic Republic and the Federal Republic of Germany, individuals wanting to merge the two sides would be in hiding, due to antipathy. He wondered if the hostility was endemic or activated by propaganda and could be reconciled. Reconciliation would be, ultimately, ecological.

He realised that if his spirit was to dominate anywhere like a lion's, it had to conserve the local inhabitants: humans, animals and plants. His central plan for a peaceful solution to the Cold War had to begin with respect for nature and for each other, by both sides. He wanted to find a place to call his own, where he would be obeyed.

CHAPTER 18
LOVE IN RUINS

Self's travels had transformed him from an engineer on holiday, into a traveller investigating national planning systems. He wanted to understand the variety of individuals and their influences in each country. He was curious about culture, history, language, geography, almost everything. He was in South America to carve a territory of governance for a thesis he could develop when he would start his PhD research on his return to the UK. His lion-sized ego was optimistic. In the thin air and serenity of the Andes, he felt like a king.

He read avidly the 'General in his Labyrinth' by Columbian writer Gabriel Garcia Marquez, a tale of the dictator Simon Bolivar's final journey from Bogota to Columbia, revealing his heroic labyrinthine memories. The magic realism of the narrative dramatically revealed unique South American conditions.

At first, Self resisted elements of fantasy with an engineer's scepticism. In time, he opened his imagination to embrace the feelings and observations of others in their spiritual realms, without qualms. He realised others' realities could differ from his own and sometimes had better explanations.

In the Galapagos, Self met a group of Americans and travelled with them for several months. They were hippies who opposed the US role in South America, especially the Monroe Doctrine, first enunciated in 1823, with elements continuing up to the present. It opposed European colonialism in the Western Hemisphere. The United States and its allies were concerned about the spread of communism, particularly in the aftermath of World War II. The policy of containment, articulated in the Truman Doctrine, aimed to prevent the further expansion of communism. It held that any intervention in the political affairs of the Americas by foreign powers was a potentially hostile act against the United States. This led to interventions and conflicts in various parts of the world, such as the Korean War and the Vietnam War. It resisted communism and socialism in South America.

His travelling companions were hippies and opposed to the US government, a view popular with some South Americans they met, who resented US political interference in their countries.

Six of them travelled together by bus to Peru, four girls and one other guy, a Frenchman. Self was feeling dominant, because when they checked into a hotel in Cuzco, one of the girls left to return to the USA, the fourth girl had taken up with the other guy and gone to their own room and he was left with two girls and one bed. The possibilities seemed to Self like a dream come true, but he knew he had to exercise self-control, because he wanted self-mastery.

He looked at the two girls. 'What happens next?' he asked.

'I am not doing group sex,' Vanessa said, tabling the idea.

'Nor me,' said Genevieve, without conviction.

So far, Self had slept only with Vanessa.

'I'm going to bed,' Vanessa said.

She lay in the middle. She and Self made love gently, trying not to let their activity and strangled cries disturb Genevieve.

The next day, their bus crawled up the steep road to the historic site of Macchu Picchu. They spent several hours looking around the ruins. Then Self led them away from the tourist centre along a little-used path up the mountainside.

'Where are we going?' asked Vanessa.

'I have a hunch we'll come to a place where we can camp,' said Self.

They came to a sign: *Entrado Prohibido*.

'They want to keep out people who speak Spanish,' Self said ironically. 'We're okay.'

They continued along a narrow precipitous track. After a two-hour trek, the overgrown path reached a hilltop, with ruins like those at Machu Picchu, although unrestored. They took off their clothes and lay on their ponchos, stark naked in the sun, with a breath-taking view over a precipitous gorge. Presently, Vanessa, Genevieve and Self made love. Self imagined he could hear the rhythms of a husky cantata played on breathy pan pipes, by Quechuan Indians. Estelle and Pierre had started together nearby, but soon they came over and joined in *a cinco*. It was sublime.

Self had an atavistic alpha desire to mate with all the females. He tried to get Estelle to join his harem, while keeping Vanessa and Genevieve away from Pierre.

'Peace, man,' he said to Pierre, when he tried to take Estelle back. 'Make like a bonobo.'

It was an extraordinary place, where he discovered spiritual truth and self-mastery. He had assumed leadership of the group and took responsibility for the others' safety, enjoying his eminence.

Self felt at home there, as if it was his own territory to command. He had responsibilities but also had control and he loved it.

He had gained respect from his knowledge of the Incas and he shared it with the others. He had researched Machu Picchu at a library in Lima. The deserted empire was discovered in 1911. The ruins were at a remote and easily defended mountain location with temples and horticultural terraces where an Incan sex cult could have existed until the 15th century. The stone walls had survived because the stone blocks had dished faces and were pegged with carved stones to hold them in position while the walls were shaken by earthquakes.

The site was abandoned after the last Incan king leapt to his death from a high place, shortly before the Spanish conquistadors arrived in Peru in 1532 and found the Machu Picchu site deserted. Disappearance of the entire population was a mystery. For every male skeleton discovered, they found eighty females.

Self was interested in community living and wanted to find out the Incan social arrangements. He was interested in communes with polygamy, having marriage to more than one spouse at a time. Polygamy was usually polygyny, in which cowives share a husband, or less often polyandry, in which co-husbands share a wife.

To explain the preponderance of female skeletons, parthenogenesis, or virgin birth without males, was extremely rare in humans, although common in over 100 species of reptiles, fish and birds. It was unlikely that the population at Machu Picchu could have been sustained without males, even by the divine intercession supposed for Jesus' conception. The Incans were peaceful and without enemies. Perhaps few males were needed to fight and they disposed of boys by infanticide.

Self wanted the social and economic conditions of socialism to cause polygamy to arise by evolution.

'Don't imagine a process of social Darwinism creating socialism,' Pierre said. 'Darwin's theory focuses on the gradual change and adaptation of species by natural selection. It's about biological processes and the diversity of life and not about the living conditions.'

The site could have been populated by a handful of high priests and many beautiful maidens brought there from all over the empire to be their servants. Such a polygynous society could easily have been ravaged by just a few Conquistadors.

Alternatively, the Spaniards could have brought diseases that afflicted the population.

For several days they camped out, reading, talking and making love, in their condor's eyrie, perched high above a verdant valley that receded into the distance, like the nave of an immense cathedral, sided by a procession of gothic arches rearing steeply from the valley floor on both sides. Self thought he could hear the thin air pulsating with Mozart's 'Requiem', played exuberantly on a pipe organ, with throbs and trills, as the light fled and shadows stole down the aisle, until with one crashing chord that reverberated the silence, the condor folded her wings and darkness settled over them.

They were careful not to pollute the site and drank water scooped up with their hands from a channel cut through the rock six hundred years before. Hunger made them high and fractious. Self tried to keep the females together with him and away from Pierre. He played on his guitar Simon and Garfunkel's haunting melody, 'El Condor Pasa'.

They were on a drugless sex-filled high, basking in the warm sun and at night clinging together under their ponchos. They had no food and on the third day, Pierre and Self dressed and descended to a village in the valley below, for provisions. As they entered the village they passed a public swimming pool. Through a fence they could see a bevy of bare-breasted women talking together at the shallow end. Trippy with hunger, they paid to go in and stripped off in a cubicle. They ran out naked, laughing, as high as kites from hunger and thin air. They jumped into the deep end. Immediately, a middle-aged man called a pool attendant, who hurried away.

They were treading water, ogling the females, when two policemen arrived and beckoned them to come to the side of the pool. They were under arrest for nakedness. The man in the water, wearing shorts, was the police chief. It turned out the 'naked' women were his family and beneath their bared breasts they wore bikini bottoms. The police handed them towels to cover themselves as they got out. Feeling foolish and scared, they put on their clothes and were escorted to the village jail, a rat-infested brick cell.

They were locked up all day, refused access to a telephone and could not inform their consulates. Eventually, with the aid of a dictionary, Self apologized formally and profusely, regretting their mistake in deducing the women were naked. Police carrying machine guns marched them along the railway tracks out of town and told them to keep going.

Hungry after a day in jail, Pierre and Self circled back to Machu Picchu and then edged their way in pitch-blackness along the narrow track etched into the mountainside, back to the girls in the ruins. Stepping off the path was likely, with a sheer drop below. Self held Pierre by his belt, as they slowly made their way along the path. It was a frightening trek and when they arrived, the others were disappointed that they hadn't brought any food.

'We are starving,' complained Vanessa, 'while you have been perving on women.'

Self was embarrassed that they had intruded on a family in a public place. It had been unintentional, foolish fun, prompted by hunger and naked breasts. They had been lucky to be treated so reasonably.

They returned along the track to Machu Picchu, where they bought food and caught a bus back to Cuzco and on to La Paz in Bolivia.

Their sojourn confirmed to Self that a strong leader could take a group to a new territory. Human nature would prefer polygamy, with either a male or female leader, but both genders could be needed to obtain food.

CHAPTER 19
CURRENCY EXCHANGE

From Bolivia, Self and three of the girls took a train from La Paz to Arica in northern Chile. Landlocked Bolivia was unable to access the Pacific coast, until a Treaty of Peace and Friendship was negotiated and a railway constructed in 1913, passing mainly through Chile.

When they arrived in Arica, the friends erected a tarpaulin tent on the beach and made a soup by boiling pippies in a can on a log fire, making a flavoursome but tough soup.

In the town, shopkeepers were boarding up their windows to avert damage expected from a demonstration protesting the Allende government, which, amid controversy, had nationalised mining companies. When Self exchanged American dollars for Chilean pesos, he received several times more than the posted rate. Local people were trying to get out of the peso, inflating the exchange rate. The travellers ate in cafés for under two dollars a day.

A majority of the Chilean people seemed to oppose the government. It was disappointing for Self, who had been excited at the prospect of a freely elected socialist government. Self's loyalty to free markets included exchanging his dollars for as many pesos as he could. He wouldn't support the regime in Santiago, when their official rate of exchange was so low. He was unable to resist the much higher black market rate.

He wanted to profit from the strength of the American dollar in Chile. He filled his rucksack with photography darkroom paper, exchanging it for dollars, at four times the official rate. He had darkroom experience and the paper seemed to be a bargain. He carried it across the border to Arequipa in Peru. There were only a couple of darkrooms there and he had difficulty finding anyone willing to buy the paper for dollars. After walking the streets between photographers' studios, he had to accept only a little more for it than he had paid in Arica.

Meanwhile in Arica, the girls had attracted a group of youths who entertained them. Strict Roman Catholic families denied the youths access to their girls and the promiscuous gringas had a magnetic effect.

Vanessa brought a young Chilean youth to meet Self.

'Will you lend him $100 to get a passport?' she said. 'He wants to go to the USA.'

'When would I get it back?' Self asked.

'He will send it to you soon, when he can.'

Self was unsympathetic. He didn't think it was his position to finance someone to leave his country, at a time when its democracy was under threat. When he checked the money he had left in their tent on the beach, one hundred dollars had been taken. The girls disappeared at the same time.

They had betrayed him and he was disappointed. His money had been grabbed unjustly, stolen by those he had thought of as his friends. A week earlier he had been with the American girls when they shop-lifted food from a supermarket, hiding it in their clothes and walking out with it. The cost was within their means and the exchange rate was favourable.

They justified their stealing as revenge against the depredation of capitalism they imagined. The stealing enabled freeloading, which Self deplored.

'Stealing is low behaviour,' Self had told them.

'Stealing from a supermarket is fair,' Genevieve said. 'Their prices are robbery.'

'They cover their costs and the owners make a profit on their investment,' Self said. 'How is that robbery?'

'The owners are wealthy capitalist pigs,' she said. 'Capitalism has to be stopped.'

'I'll buy my own food,' Self said. In his view capitalism was inevitable and worked better than state control.

The theft of his money was redistribution of his wealth, against his wishes. He didn't like it. He hadn't been offered a way to evaluate the benefit of his sacrifice, or to choose not to make it.

He never saw the money or the girls again.

Up to this time, he had admired the success of the Allende regime in Chile. He was favourably impressed that the World's first elected socialist government had devolved some power to communities.

Because US corporations in Central and South America were reported to be exploiting the local people, Self took the side of socialist agitators protesting against US intervention. There were rumours of undemocratic political events in Chile, including intervention by the CIA. Political events were disorienting and Self searched for truth, without aligning himself with either side.

Chile's experience of socialism was important for Self's consideration of having the West adopt central planning to halt the Cold War. He had been appalled by cultural discontinuities between Polish and Canadian mine planning. If the West planned like the Soviets, there was a better chance the two sides would understand each other's plans, with convergence and cooperation.

His dealing in currency exchange had bolstered his understanding of international economics. He had not yet achieved a domain of his own, except as an entrepreneur, but he was ready to become lord of a desert. As a reformer, he had to be able to consider and analyse consequences, for reform would set off chains of economic action and reaction.

Self left Chile to return to Peru. He was happy to get away unharmed. He was a hippy with a social conscience in South America, unwillingly drawn into political division.

CHAPTER 20
NATIONALISM IN PERU

Peru, like Chile and several other Central and South American countries, was dabbling in socialism in 1970 when Self was there. He wanted to distil experience of socialism and its ideological counterpart, communism, into a proposal to end the ideological struggle of the Cold War. His idea was to study for a PhD at the London School of Economics to create a centrally planned economy in the UK.

Peru had tried to develop a mixed economy like the UK's. After a successful coup d'état by the Armed Forces of Peru, the Revolutionary Government was a military dictatorship that ruled Peru from 1968 to 1980. Juan Velasco Alvarado led his government in promoting revolutionary nationalism and left-wing ideas, making a deep impact with left-leaning policies which aimed to create strong national industries to increase Peru's international independence. To that end, he nationalised entire industries, expropriated companies in a wide range of activities from fisheries to mining, to telecommunications, to power production and consolidated them into industry-centric government-run entities.

Central planning in Peru had opposition, despite dictatorship. Friction between the Velasco government and the USA was blamed for insidious violence. Peruvians assumed Self was an American and he was warned by complete strangers to be careful.

Many Peruvian people lived in dire poverty. During his 25 years, he had never seen such hardship. On the Altiplano, there were highland people living in holes in the ground, their barefoot children running beside his train carriage, begging for bones he discarded from his snack of llama chop.

Che Guevara was a medical doctor who had supported spiritually downtrodden people, suffering from poverty and tuberculosis. The following quotes are attributed to him.

It is better to die standing than to live on your knees.

I am one of those people who believes that the solution to the world's problems is to be found behind the Iron Curtain.

Man really attains the state of complete humanity when he produces, without being forced by physical need, to sell himself as a commodity.

Ernesto Che Guevara

Self usually travelled by bus. He bought tickets between cities and sometimes stayed on for days. Standing space filled with local people making short journeys. One day, when his bus was ready to depart from a terminal, he left his seat briefly to buy a chocolate bar. He asked the person in the next seat to keep an eye on his camera bag and she agreed. When he returned a few minutes later, his bag was gone. No-one had seen anything. His camera equipment was valuable. He left the bus to get help to recover it at the police station.
'You won't get that back,' said the duty officer. 'Forget about it. If you like, you can come to my house for my daughter's birthday party.'
Self went to the party, played his guitar, had a good time and forgot to grieve for his camera. It had cost more than the average annual income of a Peruvian. Without it, he was less conspicuous and his experiences of places and people was more candid. His comparative wealth had clashed with his social beliefs and he was better off without it.
Without a camera to record his travels, he focussed on the experiences of being there and recalling details from memory. Later he was able to use the internet to revive and supplement his memories.

He was self-conscious, wary of polluting local cultures with foreign values. He wanted to understand local politics but his access was restricted by his foreign identity and inadequate Spanish language ability. He was moved by the poverty he saw to want to make a difference, but lacked a domain where he could obtain experience of a truly socialist government.

He heard of a commune operating a pottery school in Lima. He had thrown pots on a wheel at school and thought he might be able to teach pottery and learn socialism. Peru was a socialist country and he expected that the school would be properly administered. But it was run by Americans, who used the school to supply adolescents with marijuana and cocaine. The commune had local teachers and they did not need him.

His experience of socialism in Peru was of desperately poor conditions, government food handouts and free education. The government had given a van for the school to use, with which they distributed drugs to youth groups. Self's experiences may not have represented all Peru, but he was unimpressed by what he had seen of Peruvian socialism. He regretted that a drug sub-economy was displacing more needed activities, such as obtaining food. Disillusioned he left Peru for Paraguay.

CHAPTER 21
NEW AUSTRALIA

Self's visit to Paraguay was to investigate a remnant of the New Australia Commune, a utopian colony founded in 1892 by William Lane, a prophet of anarchical communism. The Paraguayan Government had wanted to repopulate after the Great War of 1864-1870, when Paraguay was utterly defeated by Argentina, Brazil and Uruguay, and nine out of ten males died. They gave Lane 75,000 hectares to start an agrarian commune. In 1891, after breaking off the shearers' strike in Australia, he brought to Paraguay a shipload of 220 socialists, mainly males.

'I expect the local women made them welcome,' said Jill, who he had met in Peru and was travelling with him.

'Not at first,' Self said, reading from a handbook. 'Lane forbade the Australian men from consorting with the local Guarani women. He had with him his wife and three sons. The commune failed because the single men, were dissatisfied without women. They deserted Lane's leadership and turned for comfort to rum and the local women. In 1899, Lane quit and went to New Zealand.'

At Cosme in Paraguay, where the commune had started, they met Gabriella, a sociologist and descendant of a New Australia communist.

'The fundamental problem they had was achieving egalitarianism,' she said. 'Some people would not contribute fairly.'

'How can work be divided fairly in a commune?' asked Self.

'They have to share equally,' Gabriella said. 'A commune is defined as an intentional community of people living together, sharing common interests. They share ideals and material things.'

'How can they share?' Self asked.

'There has to be mutuality.

From each according to his ability, to each according to his needs.

Karl Marx, 1875.

'What mutual interests can they have?'

'Socialism isn't enough,' said Gabriella. 'Lane's commune lacked cohesion. Socialist communities, some as large as whole nations, may have failed for the same reason. Successful communes develop social cohesion from emotional bonding, such as religious cults, or missions, cooperatives, artisan groups, or growers and users of hallucinogenic drugs.'

'Can social bonding emerge from revolution or war?' Self asked.

'Yes, certainly,' said Jill. 'The great socialist revolutions in China, Russia, Ukraine, Yugoslavia and Cuba, built social cohesion on political ideology.'

'Is it an irony that after those revolutions, they were led by dictators?' asked Self.

'That has been a problem with socialist leaders everywhere,' said Jill. 'They didn't step down to allow democratic elections.'

'The leaders have treated the people with contempt,' Self said. 'Our visit here is revealing particularly the subservience necessary under communism and to a lesser extent under socialism.'

'It is not often highlighted,' said Jill. 'No-one wants to be subservient.'

'The great socialisms have been totalitarian and centralized, with masses atomised and subservient to the state,' Self said. 'They may have been united less by social cohesion than by fear and individual superfluity. Chile, Peru and now Paraguay have been smaller scale, less centralised and less stable.'

'If socialism fails to pay attention to individuals, there is no hope of it succeeding at a larger scale, without tyranny,' said Jill.

'I agree,' said Self. 'I had expected that a centrally planned socialist economy would be democratic. Unless we find Argentina's experience to be enlightening, it does not seem possible.'

Self had gained understanding of the different constraints on central planning in the countries he had visited. In the UK, central planning was a distant prospect.

They said farewell to Gabriela and travelled on to Argentina, in a hot bus.

CHAPTER 22
PERONISM

Self and Jill camped on the pampas at Santa Rosa, near Cordoba, in Argentina. It was an almost deserted place, by a lake and for three weeks they lived in a makeshift tent, near a hamlet and a butcher's shop, where they swam, rested and ate steaks. The grasslands were idyllic beef country and they wondered how a population with such abundant resources could have poverty and the continual conflict with their governments, complained of by Argentinians.

Local people spoke fondly of the work earlier by Eva Peron for the people, building hospitals and schools. Wife of President Juan Domingo Perón, she was First Lady of Argentina, an Argentine politician, activist, actress, and philanthropist from June 1946 until her death in July 1952. Since then she had become the legendary figurehead of a populist worker-led movement: Peronism.

'A true democracy is one in which the government does what the people want and defends only one interest: the people's. Peronism is essentially of the common people. Any political elite is anti-people, and thus, not Peronist.'
From: Juan Peron's 'Peronist Philosophy.'

Eva Peron had been the mitigating face of an authoritarian government that brought hard times to the nation. She was soft and glamorous, an impassioned speaker who won over mass rallies and international soirees. Ordinary Argentinian women could relate to the actress, who said she was working class and proud of it. She enabled them to forget their grinding poverty.

In the musical 'Evita,' the middle classes courted leaders who fawned on the aristocracy, loathing Eva, because she wouldn't parrot their beliefs. Instead, she gave ordinary Argentinians self-respect. They were proud of her as she toured European salons with her publicity machine, generating interest in trade with Argentina.

President Perón, like Velasco in Peru, was a military man who trusted organised labour., He was elected with a socialist agenda, although some said it was his wife that had won. Eva created popular reforms. Revolutionaries hijacked food trucks and like Robin Hood's band, robbed the rich to feed the poor. They drove the trucks into the slums to feed the urban starving. Five years later the unrest descended into a despotic 'dirty' guerrilla war.

Self's socialist beliefs had been upset by shortcomings of the government in Peru. He thought that for socialist programmes to succeed in the UK, the reserved and dour English would require a leader more commanding than the avuncular Harold Wilson. President Peron was egotistical and had demanded knowledge in his dealings with others. Without the subservience of the people his wife commanded, it is doubtful that his autocratic style would have succeeded. Self couldn't imagine the UK under a dominant military leader, even if the leader's spouse was glamorous and popular.

Self concluded that to succeed in the UK, a socialist revolution needed a strong and popular leader and also social bonding. Cohesive social bonding could result from an external threat, as for example when Britons faced with invasion in WWII, united. Self doubted that Cold War peril would unite Britons by cohesive socialism, when socialism was the enemy.

Self's interest in socialism for the UK was waning. When he returned to the UK, he needed a practical plan to claim his domain. There would be difficulty in achieving social bonding and moving to a centrally planned economy.

'A leader isn't able to hold a lion's territory under socialism,' said Jill, 'unless he becomes a dictator.'

'If I wanted to be a leader in a communist revolution,' said Self, 'I wouldn't do it. It is too hazardous.'

'Do you have a Plan B for the UK?' she asked.

'I'm not going to focus on reconfiguring the UK economy,' he said. 'I'll try and fix the Cold War directly.'
'Good idea.'

CHAPTER 23
GRINGO VISIT

Self was walking down a street in Buenos Aires, when he heard: 'Psst! Gringo.' When he looked around, there were several local youths, idlers, delighted to have his attention. It was a familiar scene. Gringo meant 'foreigner' and as a form of address it was derogatory. A gringo was a person, especially an American, who was not Hispanic or Latino. He was 'other'.

Self liked to blend in and here he was exposed. Although some bystander 'pssts' had an affectionate overtone, others were hostile hisses. It was partly his own fault, with hippy hair and gear, in a place where they were unusual. He was uncomfortable to be so remarked and he was irritated.

He wondered at the pay-off for his audience. Perhaps there was kudos in getting his attention, assumed American, the most powerful race on the planet. It was evidence of a cultural cringe in dealing with Americans.

On 20 July, 1969, Apollo 11's Eagle lunar module landed on the Moon. Self had watched the landing on TV, standing in a crowd before a shop window in San Salvador, in Central America. They were silent as Armstrong descended the ladder and said: 'That's one small step for man. One giant leap for mankind.'

The crowd exhaled, with sighs and relieved laughter.

Self was delighted, filled with admiration and elation. As people dispersed, he talked with a Salvadorian man, who assumed he was an American.

'Fantastico,' he said.

'Amazing,' said Self.

'Yes! You Americans are . . . like Gods!' the man said, dejectedly. 'You can do anything you want. You are great. I am nothing. I have to struggle to find food for my family. Why is there this difference between us?'

'I don't know,' Self said shrugging. 'I'm English, not American. I don't think Americans are so different, except they have money. Their success is transparent and belongs to all mankind.'

The local man shook his head, not agreeing. The Apollo program would help persuade Salvadorian diplomats to accept US hegemony in trade relations. Self doubted there would be any real benefits for poor San Salvadorians.

Self felt highly visible, regarded as an American, throughout his travels in Latin America. When he had travelled in Mexico with the hippy couple from Australia, they were watched wherever they went. At that time, protesting against the Vietnam war was building up and American hippies were popular. When the three of them grooved along in their ponchos and Stetsons, down a city street lined by office blocks, they passed a college with hundreds of students ogling them from windows. Their response was to give them the peace V sign, a wave and calling the salutation *Che'* in memory of the Marxist revolutionary Che Guevara, who was shot dead by the Bolivian Army in 1967.

There was an uproar of cheers and shouts.

Eight months later, Self was with Jill when they reached the bustling, affluent and sophisticated city of Buenos Aires. Self's excitement on reaching new places had worn off and the barrage of 'gringo' calling was annoying. He was tired of travelling and just wanted to be left alone with Jill. The stares seemed hostile. He couldn't ignore that he was in their space and he could choose to leave, blend in, or reassert his right to be there wearing his hippy clothes. He had toned down his garb but had stopped short of getting his hair cut.

He armed himself with a water pistol and squirted people who flung the word 'gringo' at him. They were too surprised to retaliate. Later he was ashamed, for attacking people who were merely showing harmless interest. He vowed never to travel without a break for so long again. It had been almost a year since he left Canada and he was tired of travelling.

When he had set off, he had wanted command of his own territory. Strangely, now when he had public acknowledgement, he didn't want it. He consoled himself that when he returned to the UK, his PhD research would create a domain where he would welcome interest with courtesy and would not be expected to be a god.

CHAPTER 24
OCEAN SPIRIT

Brazil had less social activism and turmoil than other countries on his tour. People were friendly and welcomed Jill and him. Self had timed their arrival in Rio to coincide with the Carnival in February, when the city was in party mode.

'There's a yacht race from Cape Town arriving any day,' he said. 'I want to see them come in. Maybe they'll want crew. I've always wanted to try ocean sailing.'

While they waited, they enjoyed the beaches, the music and partied at Samba schools in the favelas, where the dancers rehearsed for the Carnival parade.

'Do you want to go to South Africa?' Jill asked Self.

'Possibly,' he said. 'The favourite, Ocean Spirit, may want to sail back to the UK. That would be perfect for me.'

'What about me?' asked Jill.

'You might be able to come too,' Self said vaguely. He wasn't sure what to do about Jill, whether to continue with her. He had enjoyed being with her but her Americanness was foreign. Like other travellers from the US he had met, her ideas were more definite and better-articulated than his own and although he admired her, she was sometimes disconcerting. He wasn't sure whether the cultural differences between them would fade or magnify. He knew from friends whose international relationships had failed that intercultural romance could be hazardous.

The following day Jill received a message from Ohio, that her father had suffered a serious accident at work and might not live. She went home the next day. He saw her off at the airport, promising to keep in touch.

Self hung around the yacht club, waiting for the race to finish, so he could ask skippers for a crewing job in their onward travel.

As he stood in the crowd at the jetty, someone said 'Ship Ahoy!' and pointed. Everyone craned their necks. Visible across Guanabara Bay was the white blob of a spinnaker.

'Who is it?' someone asked.

'Ocean Spirit' a voice said. 'I'd know that spinnaker anywhere! It is Knox-Johnston's boat.'

A motor boat putt-putted out to the finishing line, with three officials standing in a row, in blazers and panamas. As the yacht crossed, a puff of smoke and the boom of a small cannon brought cheering and clapping.

Robin Knox-Johnston was a British sailor, age 32, who had teamed up with another skipper to race Ocean Spirit in the inaugural Cape Town to Rio Yacht Race. They had taken line honours, after a crossing in 23 days and 42 minutes. Two years before, he was the first person to perform a single-handed non-stop circumnavigation of the globe. Then he had won the 1970 Round Britain race in Ocean Spirit. He was already famous when they sailed from Cape Town.

Ocean Spirit was a 21.6 metres fibreglass yacht, her mizzen mast stepped forward of the rudder post, making her a ketch. She came nosing into the jetty at their feet, with the eight crew lined up along the foredeck, wearing white T-shirts, beards and glimpses of brown faces. The crowd clapped them in and stood to attention as the tinny PA system played 'God Save The Queen' and afterwards the Brazilian national anthem. The crew posed on the foredeck for news cameras, with the two skippers sitting on winches in front, flanked by the smaller men on one knee and the beefy winch men standing behind, with their muscular arms folded.

The crowd dispersed to the rowdy bar inside, with The Beach Boys harmonising the 'Sloop John B'. Self went in with them. Pushing his way through, he bought a couple of tankards of beer. He offered one to Knox-Johnston as he came in. He took it and drank deeply.

'Ah. That's great. Thank you.'

'Did you run out of beer?'

'Yes, about two weeks ago. And rum, too. We've had nothing but water since.'

'Did you have enough water?'

'Of course. We are very careful.'

'How was the race?'

'Bloody awful. We never saw another boat after the first day. No wind for days at a time.'

Self offered his hand. 'I'm Self Maidment,' he said.

They shook.

'What are you doing in Rio?' the skipper asked him.

Self told him he was an engineer and that he had been travelling.

'I hope he doesn't see I am a hippy,' Self thought. Yachtsmen and hippies were worlds apart. He had shaved, tidied up his long hair and put on a business shirt and trousers.

'Congratulations for your win,' he told him. 'Do you have a place in your crew for me? I need to get back to the UK for uni.'

'Come aboard at six bells,' the skipper told him. 'You can meet the crew.' He turned away, to talk to someone else.

That evening, Self walked up the gangplank of Ocean Spirit and met Knox-Johnson in the cabin. He briefly showed him the boat's layout and asked him to be seated.

'What time is it?' Knox-Johnson asked.

Self wasn't wearing a watch and looked at the mechanical clock on the cabin wall.

'About ten past six,' he said.

'No,' the skipper replied. 'It isn't 'about' anything. It is twelve minutes and 34 seconds past six o'clock.'

Self was taken aback.

'I don't tolerate lateness,' Knox-Johnston said. 'Crew members have exact schedules. A racing ship has to run precisely, like clockwork. I expect exactitude.'

If he had asked Self the day of the week, he would have been stuck.

'What sailing have you done?'

'Not much, just dinghy sailing at the university sailing club.'

'You would have to learn what we do quickly. What are the names of the sails?'

'Main, jib . . ..'

'Also a genoa, spinnaker and storm sails. She's a ketch, so there's another suite, for the mizzen.'

'I forgot.'

He tossed him a length of rope.

'Show me a figure-of-eight; bowline; clove hitch; and a fisherman's knot.'

Self could do a figure of eight but gave up on the others.

'I think Ocean Spirit is a bit beyond your experience at present,' Knox-Johnston said. 'You can apply again when you've done some ocean racing.'

'Thank you for considering me,' Self said lamely.

He left.

He would try and get a place on another boat. Crewing seemed servile and didn't fit with his spiritual journey and commanding his own domain. He would be going back to being a 'camel' or even a 'slave', but it would only be for the short while necessary to gain experience. Before he could command, he had to learn the ropes.

CHAPTER 25
CREW RIGHTS

The next day Self spoke to the skipper of a smaller boat lying further along the yacht club quay. Walter, about 50, was bearded and energetic. He said he had escaped from Germany before the war, by sailing, with his brother, to South Africa in a converted open lifeboat. He had lived in Cape Town for 30 years. His new yacht was clinker constructed, with the hull planks overlapping each other to add strength. She was a yawl, the mizzen mast aft of the rudder post. He had raced to Rio alone, without self-steering. When he had fallen asleep, he had drifted off course, but he had achieved a respectable position in the race. He was preparing to sail back and could use Self's help.

Self brought his pack aboard and Walter set him to filling the water containers in the bilges. The boat was basic and Self was concerned that there was not much food and little provision for safety. There was no radio. The voyage could take a month and he worried that if there was any trouble such as medical or mental problems, he could be in danger. Walter's manner was abrupt and demanding. Self spent the night aboard, but in the morning, he told Walter he had changed his mind, thanked him, shouldered his pack and went ashore.

Further around the harbour he came to the yacht Ermelo, from Durban. She had arrived three days before, several days after Ocean Spirit. The crew of eight, all men, were at work cleaning and repairing her. Self spoke to the skipper.

'Bryce Cullan,' he said, shaking hands. Self asked him if he needed crew. He invited him aboard. He was a tall, blond-haired, raw-boned South African policeman, in his thirties.

'I need to get back to the UK for uni,' Self said.

'We're going to Jamaica,' Bryce replied. 'A couple of our guys have gone to the airport. I have a couple of berths.'

'Close enough!' Self said. 'I'd love to sail with you.'

'What experience have you?'

Self told him about his dingy sailing at university.

'Ocean sailing is different,' Bryce said. 'If you learn fast you might be okay.'

A Brazilian girl, Maria, was there. Like Self she was wanting to join the crew. Bryce showed the two of them over *Ermelo*. Bryce told them he and a couple of mates had built the yacht in a backyard in Johannesburg. The cabin interior was panelled with carved woodwork recycled from a hotel and was equipped with a powerful stereo system. After their maiden voyage from Durban, the welder and the carpenter had had enough of sailing and wanted to sell their interests. Bryce was taking her to Jamaica, where he planned to run charters and earn enough to buy out the other two.

Maria had flown over from Johannesburg for Carnival. She had worked as a casino croupier. She had ideas of yacht-hopping to exotic places. Like Self, she had little sailing experience. She was young and lithe with a gamin physique, skin the colour of honey, a mop of curly black hair, a broad smile and an attractive face of Caucasian and Negroid descent. She was wearing tight-fitting jeans and a figure hugging T-shirt. She was vivacious and fun.

Bryce told them about Ermelo. She was a beamy 12 metres steel ketch, rather heavy. In the race she had finished mid-field. Self congratulated him.

Bryce introduced them to the members of the crew. There were four young men. Alan was an Englishman, the same age as Self, 25. He was a solicitor from Kensington in London and had flown down to Cape Town for the race. He had raced around Britain and was an experienced heavy weather sailor. He had gone to a famous boys' school and was social and pleasant.

Greg was a little older, a red-haired accountant from Durban. He was quiet, tall, beefy and punctilious. An experienced navigator, he had been with *Ermelo* since launching. The other two males were younger South Africans, recruited for the shake-down cruise to the Seychelles, staying on afterwards.

Self sat with Maria and the others in the cockpit, eating a lunch of sandwiches and beer. There were in-jokes that referred back to the race, which had been something of an ordeal for everyone, but was now forgotten. They were looking forward to sailing to Jamaica. Bryce was sitting next to Maria.

'Where are you going to sleep, Greg?' someone asked him.

Greg looked at Bryce.

'He can take Colin's berth,' Bryce said. Colin had flown home to look after some business.

It was a nuanced conversation and Self learned that Greg, who had been sharing the stern cabin with Bryce, was being ejected, so Maria could sleep in the only cabin with Bryce.

'Is that okay, Greg?' Bryce asked. He had a forceful manner. In earlier times a tradition on some ships was that any woman could be commandeered for the skipper's pleasure. The skipper had a lion's rights in his domain.

Self noticed that Bryce hadn't asked Maria where she wanted to sleep.

'Yes, I can use Colin's berth,' said Greg. 'But I wouldn't like to be Maria!'

There was a pin drop silence.

'What do you mean, Greg?' asked Bryce, his voice threatening.

'She won't like your snoring!' said Greg.

Everyone laughed and looked at Maria.

'If she can't take it, she'll be put ashore,' Bryce threatened. It didn't seem as if he was talking about snoring, but Maria gamely tried to ignore the threat.

'Well, it can't be too bad, or Greg would have moved already,' Bryce said. 'Alan, you haven't heard me snore from forward, have you?'

Maria laughed nervously and looked around for help.

They were wondering whether they would hear her if she called for help. The master's cabin was behind the cockpit, at the end opposite from the cabin.

Self caught her eye and gave her an empathetic smile. He felt protective of her.

'I haven't heard you snore so far,' said Alan. 'But if we do hear anything we'll be pretty pissed off. A skipper may think he has privileges, but they don't include robbing us of our beauty sleep.' Alan was saying he would not ignore any screaming from Maria. It was an oblique warning to Bryce.

'It will take more than sleep to make you beautiful, Alan,' rebutted Bryce.

'We don't want any problems with the sleeping arrangements,' said Self.

Bryce glared at him.

'What the f**k are you talking about?' he said, threatening.

'You know what I mean,' said Self.

Maria's rights would be defended by Self and Alan. At last Self had a domain of his own to protect from a usurper. His lion spirit had taken a long time to be provoked but was ready to fight. When wild lions fight to access females, the loser is usually physically and psychologically injured and leaves the pride. Fighting is avoided if the defender accepts domination and backs down.

When lunch was over, Bryce made an announcement.

'Maria and Self, you know your berths,' he said. 'You can get your stuff and spend the night aboard. In the morning, we've some provisioning, repairs and cleaning to do. We'll sail on the high tide at noon. Tonight, we'll have sundowners.'

CHAPTER 26
SAIL LOCKER

Self and Maria fetched their things and stowed them. As the Sun lowered, everyone assembled in the cockpit. The Sun dived and was gone, leaving Rio aglow on the horizon. Bryce poured a tot of rum apiece.

Self played on his guitar and sang 'The Times They Are A-changing'. The others, not being sympathetic to the youth revolution, listened unmoved. However, they joined in lustily when he sang: 'Michael Row The Boat Ashore' and 'Sister Help To Trim The Sail'.

Bryce interrupted.

'Do you know 'Sloop John B'?'

Self played the arpeggio chords of the sea shanty and they all sang, *con gusto*.

Self was relieved that Alan would help protect Maria if Bryce attacked her. The two South African guys seemed to have no objection to Bryce's racism, as if it was normal in South Africa. They wouldn't go against Bryce, who acted tough.

Then there was telling of stories, some of them tall ones. Bryce poured another tot of rum apiece. He told how he had implemented the apartheid laws in Johannesburg, brutalizing black men and black women. Bryce was fiercely proud of his white ascendency and derogated blacks.

Self respected the skipper's right to air his sexism and racial bigotry on his own boat, so he let them pass. He would confront him if he denied Maria's right to decline sex with him. Self and Alan were provoked, shaking their heads, scowling. He told story after story of his bigotry, until Self spoke to him.

'Would you stop talking about hurting black people,' Self said. 'It is cowardly to mistreat people when they have no defence.'

'They got what was coming to them,' Bryce replied dismissively.
Self led them singing the Times Are Changing.

Afterwards, Greg passed up from the galley dinners of pies and baked beans. They ate, sang for another hour and drank more rum. The guys disappeared to their bunks below, leaving Alan and Self with Bryce and Maria. Bryce tried to put his arm around Maria, but she moved away. Self kept the chat going, giving Bryce time to sober up. Eventually Bryce told Maria to turn in, so she would not disturb him later. The two went to the captain's cabin like Little Red Riding Hood and the Big Bad Wolf.

Alan and Self drank together.

'Let me know if you hear anything in the night,' Self told Alan.

'You too,' said Alan.

They went below.

Self's hammock in the smelly forward cabin was underneath another, without much headroom. He lay there planning what to do about Bryce.

The skipper was an autocrat and bully. Bryce was bigger and by his own account a hardened fighter. If there was a confrontation, Self would avoid violence if possible.

In the morning, Bryce was up early with the rest of the crew, but there was no sign of Maria. Self hadn't heard her in the night.

'Where's Maria?' Self asked Bryce.

'Below,' he replied.

The crew prepared the yacht to sail at noon. They laid out all the sails to dry in the Sun, folding them carefully and stored them in the sail locker, with the eye of each sail uppermost, ready for a shackle to haul it aloft. They topped up the water tanks and cleaned the head and galley. They stowed the fresh food and booze brought by Bryce. Then they washed the decks and went to the clubhouse for their last showers.

When everything was shipshape, they untied the mooring ropes and motored out, hauling up the sails as they went. When they had exited the channel, Bryce turned off the diesel. As they reached out into the Atlantic, they turned northwards, heading downwind. They could hear the slosh of the bow wave, with gurgles from the keel and the creak of taut sheets. They all sat together along the starboard gunwale, watching Corcovado Peak dwindle away, with its white statue of Christ, arms outstretched. For Self, this was an adventure of a lifetime.

Maria emerged on deck in the afternoon, with a black eye. When Bryce went below for something, she sat beside Self in the cockpit and whispered to him: 'He hit me. Unless I have sex with him he's going to put me ashore in Recife. I don't have any money.'

She was pale, scared by the monstrous Bryce.

Bryce came up and saw her talking to Self.

'How are you two getting along?' he asked Self.

'Maria tells me you hit her,' Self said. 'When I get off this boat I will seek an International Citizens Arrest Warrant from the International Common Law Court of Justice.'

Bryce was taken aback. He thought Self was joking.

'Ha-ha.'

'I'm serious,' said Self. 'You can't hit people.'

'It was an accident,' Bryce scowled. 'You need to keep your hippy eyes focussed on your sailing, or you won't ever get to where you want to go. It can get pretty rough out here. Accidents happen. We're in international waters. There's no law here and people can do what they like.'

It was an ugly threat. Maria was in danger and so was Self, if he helped her.

'She has human rights and International Court Law applies,' Self asserted. 'You keep your hands off her. She is not going to sleep in your cabin anymore. She'll sleep in a crew hammock when he's on watch.'

'So what will happen when he comes off watch?'

'She'll change to another hammock.'

'You're kidding!' Bryce laughed. 'I don't believe you would turn her out of your hammock. You would climb in with her. You want her, don't you? Why should the black bitch be with you, when this is my boat? She will have to sleep in the bow locker, with the door closed so the guys can get some privacy changing their gear.'

The bow locker was a small cupboard.

'It's full of sails,' Alan said. 'There's no ventilation.'

'The door is slatted and she can sleep on top of the sail bags,' said Bryce. 'I'm not having her take the crew's minds off their jobs. She'll soon come back to my cabin. You'll see.'

Maria shook her head. 'I'll try the sail locker,' she said.

'Well that's settled for the moment,' Bryce said. 'When we get to Recife, you get off.' He turned to Self: 'And you too. You keep out of my way.'

Self was dismayed that Bryce perceived him as a threat to his command, as if Self was contesting his dominion. He could have to find another way to get home.

CHAPTER 27
STORM

That evening, while the others tried to rest in their bunks, with waves pounding against the hull, it was Bryce and Greg's watch. They had full sail on both masts, taut and vibrating. As the wind veered to westerly, its speed increased and they changed course to a broad reach to prevent the genoa tearing. It was dark when they heard Bryce's cry 'All hands on deck.'

Pulling on clothing, they scrambled up the cabin steps. The shock of the wind blast almost knocked them off their feet.

'Take down the genoa and put up jib number 2. Reef the main and mizzen.'

With Bryce at the helm, the six crew lowered the genoa and wound it around its halyard, tying the roll neatly along the starboard lifeline. They tied folds in the main sail to the boom, reefing it. Maria helped wrap the mizzen sail around its boom.

The wind was too strong to stay on a beam reach and they headed Ermelo out into the South Atlantic. Their course now lay across empty ocean to West Africa. They went below, stripped off their wet gear and tried to resume their sleep, but the shock and noise of waves pounding on the forward hull was jarring and prevented relaxation.

At midnight, Maria joined Alan and Self for their watch. Alan showed them how to steer a compass bearing and trim the sails.

They were running before a stiff wind and Ermelo was overtaken by four metre waves, lofting spray over them. About 4 am they called the others up for another sail change, putting up jib number 3, which was smaller and they were on a more even keel.

Self stood with his legs apart at the helm, keeping her sighted on a distant cloud behind the bowsprit, selected within a few degrees of a convenient compass bearing. They were moving fast, over-taking the white horses of foam on the waves they crested and sailed down, cleanly and efficiently. The wind seemed like a blessing, given freely, without after effects. Their voyage was perfection.

Self, Alan and Maria had the watch from midnight to 8.00 am. At 8.00 am the two young South African guys took over, tying safety lines around their waists and clipping them to halyards to be able to move about on deck, while being pummelled by waves and gusting gale force winds.

Self lit the stove and put on the frying pan. Although the ship was hard over, the stove swung on a gimbal and stayed level. He passed up to the others in the cockpit bowls with breakfast, fried eggs, bacon and sausages. Cooking was uncomfortable for him and he felt seasick. He went up to the cockpit, leaving Alan with the cooking. When he had a horizon to focus on, he felt better. Maria rinsed off the bowls in a bucket of seawater. After breakfast, their watch retired below, with Alan and Self in their hammocks and Maria in the sail locker.

Self slept most of the day. On Bryce and Greg's watch the wind stiffened. Ermelo's bow regularly buried in waves, crashing water onto her foredeck, washing over her entire length. Self worried that the bows might stay buried and they would all be washed away, but Ermelo always reared up again, porpoising through the waves. Self was thankful to be aboard a strong steel vessel. Greg was at the helm, lashed to the compass binnacle, held by a harness to stop him being carried away. They had to yell to hear each other, but the roar of breaking waves prevented all but basic understanding.

When the jib threatened to capsize them, they replaced it with the storm jib, number 4, their smallest sail, made of fabric as thick as a board. They became more upright, screaming down huge waves, without sufficient wind pressure to hold her straight, about to broach, with the rudder above the sea surface and the helmsman unable to steer. If she broached, the mast could snap and they might die.

Self's earlier feeling of control disappeared. He sensed several times that his life hung by a thread. He had never been in a storm at sea before and he was astonished by the height and power of the waves. There was no regular pattern. They came from every direction, as if determined to roll Ermelo over and sink her. He tried to focus on the waves one at a time, trusting that the storm would abate.

On their next shift, Alan stabilised their flight by tying a sea anchor to the stern pulpit. It was a canvas drogue, on a long line like a parachute, which filled with water and dragged behind them. It held them straight with the waves as they rolled past, with the westerly wind on her superstructure and on the tiny storm jib, propelling them towards Africa.

'What will we do when we reach land?' Self asked Alan.

'Hopefully, the storm will have blown out by then. We have some way to go.'

Slowly the storm receded. In an epiphany, Self realized that in tough conditions, people are essentially unequal but expected to do their best to help the group survive, with no place for freeloaders. They looked after themselves, without endangering others. The leaders, Bryce, Alan and Greg, sacrificed their own safety to help others.

After four days the storm died away. They didn't know where they were, but figured they were halfway to West Africa.

'That's enough running. Let's try and beat northwest,' Bryce said.

The wind had dropped and they hauled in the sea anchor, took down the storm jib and hoisted jib number 2, heading back the way they had come.

For two days and nights they were on a beam reach, going fast, careering down long rolling waves. It was exhilarating. Their spirits were high from surviving the storm, but they were exhausted. They quickly recovered and began enjoying themselves. On Self's watch the three of them chatted through the night, getting to know each other, under the vaulted Milky Way. They watched constellation Orion rise in the east, pass overhead and set in the west. The vastness of the Universe made their bobbing progress seem serenely insignificant. In their wake, turquoise bioluminescence sparkled in wavelets. Their nights on watch were an antidote to Self's former subservience, encouraging him to value his own uniqueness and self-mastery.

'I wish this night will go on and on forever,' said Maria.

'Me, too,' said Alan. 'I feel like stardust, blown through space, my destiny unknown, and there is nothing I can do to change it. Going with the flow is sweet surrender.'

'I never noticed the Milky Way before,' Self said. 'I didn't think it mattered, like wallpaper. There was no point in looking at it, because it was too distant to matter.'

'And now?' asked Maria.

'Staying alive is not so important to me now,' he said. 'The milky way shows me that I am not at the centre of my life. If fate deals me a losing hand, too bad. But I would like to reach my goals, have a career and a family.'

'What about you, Alan?'

'I go forward one day at a time,' Alan said. 'I want to make a difference to my family, friends and strangers, too. The more people and more difference I make, the more successful I will be.'

'He sounds like a politician on the stump,' Self said to Maria. 'What about you?'

'I do not have much ability to change the world outside me,' she said. 'I will be content when I die if I have acted wisely for myself and the people near me and have done the best I can with what I have, without hurting others.'

'You are humbler and kinder than Alan and I,' Self said. 'I wish the best will come your way.' He liked her very much.

'Where are we?' asked Maria, after they had sailed northwest for several days.

'We have no ship to shore radio to give us a fix,' said Alan.

'How can we find out?' she said.

'I'll ask Greg if he can get a sunshot,' said Alan.

Greg carried the exotic sextant on deck and took it out of its case. It would measure the angle of the Sun above the horizon. The measurement had to be made from a known deck elevation, at a known temperature, at precisely noon GMT. He tuned the radio to the BBC's World Service.

'The pips are broadcast every hour,' he said. 'The sixth pip marks a new hour. I'll take a shot at noon, if she's steady enough.'

Greg read the angle and looked up their latitude in an almanac.

'We're about 15 degrees South,' he said, pointing to a horizontal grid line. 'It's this latitude line on the chart. Because we have sailed for 6 days at an average of about 9 knots, we are 2400 kilometres from Rio, I'll draw a circle at that radius and find where it intersects.' He inscribed a circle on the chart.

'We're here.'

He pointed to a position near the centre of the South Atlantic, more than halfway to St Helena, a British overseas territory 4000 kilometres east of Rio.

'To get to the Caribbean, we can head northwest, passing near Recife in Brazil.'

'Are you sure that's where we are?' Bryce had joined them on deck.

'No, I'm not sure,' said Greg. 'We won't be able to check it until we see land.'

'Could we run into land before then?' asked Self.

'Yes,' said Bryce. 'There are islands slightly south. We need to keep a lookout 24 hours, during every rostered watch.'

With the wind brisk and abeam, it was delightful. Ermelo flew across the water.

Self, Alan and Maria spent four nights on watch together, talking under the Milky Way.

They could have used their time together chatting about trivia, but they talked about the Universe, philosophy and themselves. Conditions were right to reflect on the big picture, their lives and their futures. They got to know each other's innermost selves, understanding each other and wanting always to stay friends.

CHAPTER 28
IDEALISM

'What research will you do at university?' Maria asked Self, sitting together in the cockpit, as Ermelo rolled along under the stars.

'I'm not sure yet,' Self told her and Alan, also in the cockpit. 'I was going to find out whether the UK economy could achieve more equality by central planning. But Peru, Chile and Argentina have tried central planning and inequalities have continued.'

'Maybe central planning doesn't help with equality?' said Maria.

'There has to be growth,' said Self. 'It is easiest to give out equal portions from a large pie. The largest pie results when everyone strives their hardest from self-interest. The combined achievement can be a vast resource. Adam Smith described a baker as benefiting his community, in the best way possible, by supplying bread for his profit. People have to be allowed to strive for themselves. When there is growth, it can be shared equally. Without growth, sharing can take away previous shares from people and is more difficult.'

'I think you are saying that if the shares are unfair, people won't try as hard as they could?' said Alan.

'They won't,' Self said. 'Most people try hardest for themselves and their relations. Equality is rewarding and sets up healthy competition between equals. People are capable of performing extraordinary feats, like surviving storms, crossing oceans, or burying the hatchet. Sharing has to be devolved. Centralisation is remote and the centre usually takes more than it gives.'

'It is the principle of subsidiarity,' said Alan. 'Every issue should be decided at the lowest level that involves all those who are affected.'

'Subsidiarity could want the lion's territory to be devolved,' Self thought. *'I won't be able to dominate my territory. I could have to share it.'*

'It requires that each person or group of persons should be given the space to do everything for themselves which they are capable of doing, with autonomy and dignity,' said Alan.

'It looks at the problem of how to delegate from the viewpoint of the person delegated, rather than seeking affirmation by a controlling authority,' said Self. 'I like it. People are encouraged to do their best.'

'I like it too,' said Maria. 'Even on this yacht, where our skipper coordinates, the crew members can have autonomy and dignity. The old sailing ships had tyrannical captains and enslaved crews who worked inefficiently, with fighting, ill health, disobedience and mutiny. On a ship, as in other workplaces, subsidiarity seems like the oxygen of group performance.'

Self's spirit now wanted to share a territory with people united by self-interest. His interest in centrally sponsored pottery communes and social programmes had gone. Yachting had imbued him with individualism. Although most shipboard tasks served the community, such as preparation of food and gear, they were supervised by the best qualified crew members, who took on responsibilities, rather than waiting for the skipper to assign them.

It was a turnabout from orthodox socialism and he knew he had to adjust his research plans. He had investigated central planning during his travels, but his interest had turned to individualism.

'I'm not sure how individuality can hold sway when there is slaving to be done,' Self said.

'Workers can specialize, with their qualification controlled by professions,' Alan replied.

'That would be a transition from the slavery of the herd to feudalism, like contracted labour under capitalism,' Self said.

'It looks like you won't be researching central planning for the UK, then,' said Alan. 'There are too many feudals.'

'Haha. No, I'm more interested in devolution of planning from central government to regional or other lower levels, by granting workers authority at that level.'

'Why not decentralize?' asked Alan.

'Decentralisation asks lower individuals to accept responsibility without giving them authority to act. It puts them in an impossible situation. Devolution of power is better because it grants the authority needed for independent action.'

'It would be a revolution in the UK,' Alan said. 'You will make enemies of those in power, but you could win over independent workers and small businessmen.'

'You're right. Political representatives will resist allowing lower level control,' Self said.

'The irony of electing leaders is that they can abuse their power,' Alan said. 'It's an inconvenient truth. Are you an anarchist?'

'No,' said Self. 'Anarchy doesn't have authority or controlling systems. There has to be some responsibility. I want it devolved to persons appointed by democracy, enabled to use their skills.'

'That's the leadership problem again,' Alan said. 'Most leaders don't want to devolve. They would have less to do, with lower status and would receive less pay. They are unlikely to implement devolution.'

'Perhaps the subordinates could hold the bosses to account to devolve authority to those responsible.'

'You're an optimist,' replied Alan, 'if you believe subordinates can take responsibility.'

'They should be able to take as much as they want,' said Self.

They had passed another night talking under the stars and Self had realised the kernel of a solution to the Cold War could be devolution implemented from the bottom up.

CHAPTER 29
CAPSIZED

On the sixth day, the storm petered out and there was a shout 'Land Ahoy' from Maria on the night watch in the bow. They could see distant lights ahead, along a low coastline with a hill.

'It's Cabo Sao Roque, the most easterly point of South America,' said Alan.

'It's just above Recife,' said Bryce, coming on deck. 'There's a sailing club. We can go in there and get a beer and a shower.'

Recife was on the northern side of the great Amazon River estuary, 50 kilometres wide in the wet season. The water they sailed on had become murky. The port was too shallow for Ermelo's keel and they anchored two kilometres out from shore. All seven of them squeezed into the ship's dinghy. Maria wanted to take her pack ashore and leave, but Bryce told her there wasn't enough room for it in the dinghy.

'You can come back with us and bring it over tomorrow,' he told Maria.

He seemed to be backing down on wanting her to leave. She had kept out of his way, made herself useful and was well-liked by the crew.

'Bryce should apologise to her,' said Self to Alan.

'South African policemen don't apologise,' he said.

Self hadn't crossed swords with Bryce again and hoped he had forgotten his threat to put him ashore too.

Alan, their best oarsman, rowed them to the Recife Yacht Club.

They lunched at the club. Then they helped Bryce carry supplies from a supermarket to the dinghy. Most of it was cans of beer. There was hardly room for everything and they sat on the supplies with about two centimetres of freeboard.

'Steady! You'll have us in the water!' warned Alan.

They were quite drunk and sang 'Barnacle Bill the Sailor' at the top of their voices: 'Who's that knocking at my door, said the fair young maiden' followed by the rest of the lewd ditty. When they were about halfway back to Ermelo, Self spied a standing wave, pouring water down in slow motion, like a river bore, except this was in open water a kilometre from shore. A standing wave was thought to be formed by a wave reflecting off a boundary, before it moved in the opposite direction. The original wave and the reflected wave were supposed to interfere and create a stationary wave. None of them had ever seen the phenomenon before.

Self was fascinated by the perpetual motion, an impossible technological dream for an engineer.

'Let's get a closer look,' he said.

Alan rowed them towards it, when suddenly, a wave reared up from under a flat sea and dumped them. The dinghy filled with water, turned over and was carried away on a breaking wave, leaving them treading water surrounded by groceries and bobbing cans of beer. They were a kilometre from Ermelo. The shore was about a kilometre the other way, a demanding swim.

'Self, you're a f**king idiot,' said Bryce.

Without a word, the guys set off swimming for the shore. Self started to follow, then he heard Maria call faintly.

'Help! I can't swim!'

She was clinging to an oar, trying to keep her head above water. Self swam over to her and held her in a lifesaving position, floating on her back with her head on his chest. He told himself not to have sexual designs on this girl. He felt privileged to be able to help her.

'Thank you,' she said.

Having only the experience of one school lesson in lifesaving, Self began backstroking with one arm and kicking steadily. It was a long way and he had to take rests.

He wondered for a moment why it had fallen to him to rescue her. Perhaps the other guys' were not strong swimmers, or maybe they were too drunk to care for anyone except themselves.

He changed his backstroke to the other arm for a while and then back again.

He was getting tired. He got Maria to hold onto his shoulders from in front, with her body under his as he swam breaststroke. It was slower but easier. He asked her to help him by kicking. Feeling her lithe body moving under his was exciting and he wanted her. She would be able to feel him against her and he wondered if she was aroused too. She smiled at him. He looked away to hide his embarrassment.

There was a shout from ahead, and he trod water to see. One of the guys was waving, pointing along the shore to the right.

'Oil,' he shouted. 'Go around.'

Just their luck. An oil slick. He turned and followed him, going parallel to the shore. The guy ahead kept on swimming without getting closer to shore and Self was getting desperate. He was tired and coughing, trying to clear water from his lungs. Thinking he might not make it, he headed for the beach through the oil. His arms were coated with black goo, with an oily taste in his mouth. The oil was thick with globs sticking to Maria's hair. He cursed whoever spilled it. It was in his eyes and they were bleary. He took his direction from the Sun. His limbs were heavy with exhaustion and he could hardly stroke. He was thinking he was finished, when a wave lifted them, then another and another. Maria was torn from his grip and they were dumped by a breaker. She disappeared beneath the surface. Frantically he swam until he touched her with his foot and pulled her up to the surface, both of them coughing weakly. Then he felt a beach underfoot and crawled up onto the sand, where he collapsed.

The others came and looked at them, covered with black filth.

'They won't let you into the sailing club like that,' said Bryce.

'Nor you into the life-saving club,' Self said nastily.

'Aren't we the big hero?' the skipper sneered. 'Guess who you want in your hammock tonight?'

Maria looked at him and scowled but said nothing.

CHAPTER 30
LAID UP

The crew walked along the beach to the sailing club. Maria and Self were covered in petroleum and stayed outside while the guys went in. Alan came out with a couple of buckets, some rags, a bar of soap and a bottle of diesel.

'Diesel? Hell!' said Self. 'Don't they have any liquid detergent or turps?'

'No. Sorry, this is all they have.'

He had used diesel on the farm to clean his hands and arms after working on engines. It wasn't much good as a skin cleaner – too oily – but better than nothing. After using it, his skin hurt. It was mid-afternoon and the sun was fierce, frying him. They stayed by the tap, cleaning themselves, but there was no shade. Self had sunburn through his T-shirt, from sailing under the noonday sun near the Equator. By the time he was reasonably clean, he felt pinpricks all over and was nauseous with a throbbing headache. Maria seemed to be okay. Her dark skin wasn't sunburnt like his.

Bryce bought more groceries to replace those they had lost. A local yachtie took everyone back to *Ermelo* in his runabout, then found their dinghy and brought it back.

That evening, Self went to his hammock, alternately vomiting, sweating profusely and shivering. His head was thumping and he took some aspirin. He wanted to shit, but ever since boarding *Ermelo* a week previously he had been constipated. Alan told him boats affect some people that way.

As he lay in his hammock, Self's reality merged with fantasies. He imagined Bryce was a lion and he was contesting his domain, trying to take Maria away from him. Although Bryce had mistreated Maria, he wasn't all bad. He had saved all their lives on Ermelo. Perhaps life and death dramas make yacht skippers into bullies.

Next morning, Maria collected her things and Alan rowed her ashore. She was going to Sao Paolo for a visit with her family. Self lent her $30 for the bus fare; she would send it to him in England.

'Good luck,' he said, hugging her.

'Thank you for saving me,' she said simply. 'Get well soon.'

With a hug, she was gone, with all her belongings in a kitbag over her shoulder. She left a piece of paper in his hand. It was her addresses, in Brazil and in South Africa. He had happy memories of her but felt he had missed something good.

Self-returned to his hammock and thought he was dying. Everything was fuzzy and distant.

Alan returned with the dinghy. The others raised the anchor and Ermelo set off for Jamaica.

In his hammock, Self was delirious and didn't know where he was. Greg took his temperature. It was dangerously high.

'He needs a doctor,' Greg said.

Bryce came down to his bunk and stared at him balefully.

'We can't get a doctor out here,' he said.

'Can we go back to Rio?' asked Alan.

'Three days sail? Not for this useless hippy,' Bryce said. 'It was his fooling around with his impossible dream wave that capsized us. Serves him right. If he dies, we'll slip him over the side when the others are asleep and no-one will be any the wiser.'

'You can't do that!' exclaimed Alan.

'Just watch me,' Bryce said.

Self heard him and gathered all his remaining strength to make a recovery. He sat up in the cockpit shivering.

Bryce's hammock-side visit frightened Self. Alan, recognising he was dehydrated, brought mugs of water and bathed him with a wet sponge. It was heat stroke. Self alternated between unconsciousness and incoherence.

After about three days he began to feel better. He lurched up to the cockpit for sundowners. They gave him a big hand.

'That's the best imitation of dying I've ever seen,' said Bryce callously.

'With all that diesel in you, your farts will ignite,' someone joked.

'Ha ha.'

'Have you had a shit yet?' asked Alan.

'Yes,' he smiled.

'Alleluia!'

Self sat in the cockpit getting better, as they rolled along on a broad beam reach.

A week later they arrived at Trinidad's Port of Spain yacht club. Self said his goodbyes and took a plane home to the UK. It was an abrupt end to a year of travel. Heat stroke had knocked his metabolism off centre and he needed to lie up and recover. He expected his parents to forgive his infrequency of correspondence and put him up in England.

After a week in Somerset and his mother's cooking, he was right as rain. He went up to London to start a PhD.

Self's quitting from Continental disappointed his father. He had been proud to have a son working as an engineer. Self was unable to persuade him that ending the Cold War was more glorious than petroleum engineering.

'I'm one for believing you should stick to what you're good at,' his father said. 'What you're getting into is different from what you have been doing and you might not win.'

'Nothing ventured, nothing gained,' Self replied.

'Pride comes before a fall,' warned his father.

Self reviewed his progress in finding a solution to the Cold War. His achievements were modest. He had achieved a confident understanding of the roots of corporate and government behaviour. In Canada, Self had been an engineer in virtual slavery doing some of the heavy lifting for his work group. He had quit to become a hippy traveller.

He had been a socialist hippy at first, but with declining interest in group welfare and growing self-mastery he had become a libertarian. After a month before the mast and surviving the storm his attention was focussed on his independent needs, leaving others to care for themselves.

He had been drawn instinctively to crewing on a yacht and asserted self-mastery in protecting Maria from Bryce and saving her from drowning. It was ironic that his interest in renewable energy had led to capsizing of their food supply, parodying the situation in some developing countries, like India. He adopted devolution as an ideal for libertarian minimisation of the state's encroachment on individual rights. He would try to develop a devolution thesis for stopping the Cold War.

Self worried about news of military escalation and enlargement of the missile arsenals of the Soviets and Western Allies. The world was living in the shadow of a nuclear Armageddon. No-one seemed to be working for peace.

'Let me be in time,' he thought.

PART 5

DRAGON

When he returned to the UK he wanted to create a new paradigm of superpower planning devolved to border locations where the Soviet bloc countries and the Western powers had begun interacting. Religious, social and cultural exchanges could end the Cold War impasse, which had existed since 1945.

In the space where peace could grow, Zarathustra's universal spiritual truth was a contest in which the lion's will to power clashed with the existing lord, the dragon..

'I will,' roared the lion, demanding a sacred rejection of dragon culture. 'Thou shalt,' the dragon snarled fiercely, defending the moral laws and traditions that maintained the confrontation. Their opposition was preordained as a part of Zarathustra's universal truth. Nietzsche had consigned the religion, morality, traditions and history espoused by the dragon to a rubbish bin, but the lion spirit had to fight with the dragon for his will to prevail and it was not done easily.

Self wanted to build self-mastery and dominion on his own terms. These included having intimate relations and children with the dragon, a female. But she asserted old moral laws and societal values he disdained. The lion and dragon exerted opposite influences on their offspring. She wanted to vanquish his spirit. Self sought to slay her, figuratively, opposing her with all his might, but could not prevail.

CHAPTER 31
IMPERIAL COLLEGE

The Cold War had scarred Self's youth and was still menacing when he returned to the UK, at 25. There were news reports every day that the USA and USSR had added missiles to their arsenals, escalating the conflict. Soviet citizens were being shot escaping over the Berlin Wall. The sides seemed implacably opposed, with nuclear Armageddon and a holocaust imminent.

Self began research for his PhD at Imperial College, in London, aiming to find a solution to the Cold War. He had considered enrolling at the London School of Economics, where he could have studied socialism within the discipline of sociology. He chose Imperial College, to align himself more closely with free individualism and capitalism. He wanted collectives to be devolved that retained capitalism's individual initiative and independence. He was more likely to find a solution with those characteristics at IC than at LSE.

A problem was that he lacked a progenitor, familiar with his field of interest. The weakness of his supervision was not apparent to him immediately. Self had a penchant for independence and he was solipsistic - a Boomer, self-absorbed, irreverent and amoral. He was content to read and read, undirected, convinced he was making progress. Sometimes it worked and he discovered something but more often he found nothing.

He met Gretchen, a postgraduate studying feminist theory at Bedford College for women at London University. She was an Australian, of the Silent Generation, moral and dutiful in defending traditional values. Her spirit seemed to balance his and she moved into his flat. He was preoccupied with establishing a research domain. She made herself useful, in a sycophantic way

He had not yet realised her hostility towards him but she began to treat him with contempt. He had no obligation to her and she began to assume he had. She expected him to tell her he loved her, when he transparently did not. He wanted her to leave.

She stood at the front door with a packed suitcase.

'If you don't agree to marry me, I'm leaving,' she said.

She wanted him to be responsible for their relationship, which wasn't working, levering him into permanency he didn't want. Her tenacity in seeking marriage caught him by surprise. A true marriage has willing partners. Instead of leaving, she manipulated a false marriage. Several men had misled her and deserted her, as if this excused her treating Self aggressively, with contempt.

Not to seem ungrateful for the effort she had made, he didn't reject her when he should have. Losing no time, she connived their marriage with his family, whose reflex was to domesticate him with their morality, at a time when he was too preoccupied with his work to actively oppose a wedding. His catatonic non-participation in the ceremony was overlooked. Their marriage went ahead in haste, which he regretted afterwards, when Gretchen began blocking his freedom.

The marriage ended his self-mastery. He realised too late Gretchen was inspired, by Germaine Greer and others, to get what she wanted from men

She said YES to starting a family immediately after the wedding.

'NO,' he said. 'You agreed not to have a baby until I have finished my PhD. A baby would demand more time than I can afford.'

'I did not agree to that,' she said.

'I remember that you did. There will be no baby until I have finished.'

He was in no doubt that having a baby would sabotage his PhD. He was already stressed and had a premonition that having a baby would be his undoing.

'If I don't have a baby soon, it may be too late,' she nagged.

Next, Gretchen tried to overturn her agreement.

'I want to have a baby,' she said, demanding.

A baby would disrupt the concentrated effort necessary. Until he saw her write her birth date in the marriage register, he had thought her age was as she had told him, the same as his. But she was 30, several years older, of an age regarded in those days as 'elderly', supposedly too old for child bearing, because older mothers were said to be more at risk of having babies with birth deformities, disabilities and congenital defects. Now Gretchen seized on the myth to hasten the pregnancy he did not want.

Constrained by the truth of her age, he would not have married her. Her haste to have a baby followed from her lying about her age.

'No baby until my research is done!' he said. 'You agreed before we married.'

'Oh, phooey! What does that matter? A PhD certificate won't get us a better life.'

'A PhD is necessary for the academic career I want. A baby now would be a huge distraction.'

Gretchen was desperate to have a baby while she still could.

'Every day of delay increases the risk that I will be unable to conceive. You should quit uni and get a job.'

'Her treachery is disloyal,' Self thought. *'I can't finish with her because separating now would be upsetting at a time when I have to concentrate on my PhD. My mistake has been to marry a woman who is wrong for me.'*

When he told Nick about her hostility, he was unsympathetic.

'It is a common predicament,' said Nick. 'Nietzsche allegorized your situation in his book 'Thus Spake Zarathustra.' Your Gretchen is malicious like the dragon in the story.'

Self read the fable of the Camel, Lion and Child with dismay. The dragon did not prefigure everything about Gretchen, but she began to assume a place in his life like the dragon in the Zarathustra story. If he had known Gretchen would be so opposed to his ambitions, he would not have taken up with her. She had positive characteristics that enabled him to live with her for thirty three years but their relationship progressively degenerated and in the end she left him.

It is not unusual for couples to grow apart but he and Gretchen were opposed from the start. She had contrived their marriage and children, when they should have stayed apart.

He realised from Gretchen's behaviour that he was afflicted with a fierce dragon with a reflex commitment to his downfall. In the same way electrical charges and action forces have polar opposites, she was his negative and the forces between them could unbalance and overthrow his positive lionship. Zarathustra's story apprised them of atavistic zero sum competition between lions and dragons.

According to the theory of philosopher Derrida, a positive lion concept could naturally be opposed by a negative dragon. Their inherited genetic types had been honed into binary opposites by a shared ancestral environment. They were irreconcilable, unable to complement or appease each other. When describing the characters of the two and negatives of one was mentioned, the reality was they were both culpable of acrimonious feuding.

He would gain little from complaining about her but he wanted to stem the tide of her intrusion into his life. He hoped that she would cease her attacks and he would be able to resume control of his life. But she continued to press him at every opportunity, like a chess player who keeps his opponent on the ropes by repeated checking.

They were deadlocked for months. The dragon was reneging on her promise to refrain from child-bearing and the lion was scrambling to create a thesis with an early finish date for a PhD.

CHAPTER 32
SOCIETY GAME

Self's head of department at Imperial College sent him on a week-long workshop, to gain experience of organisation dynamics.

'Maidment, if you are going to bring change to organisations, you need to understand how they work,' the professor said. 'This workshop is an opportunity to experience organisation roles you will come across.'

The venue was Kings College, at Cambridge University, with its crumbling stonework, quadrangles and manicured lawns. There were 250 PhD students, gathered from far and wide to play games together, tutored by staff from the London Graduate Business School. They dined in the college, experiencing the college life of Britain's elite. Self reached his room through cloisters and up a circular stone staircase. His window was mullioned, with tiny panes, overlooking a grassed quadrangle. The elite ruling there was well established.

On the first day, they played a war game 'Escalation' in groups, simulating Cold War negotiation and deception strategies. On the second morning, they all gathered in the Great Hall for a role play game, called 'Society'. A professor who said he was the King instructed them. It was supposed to be a microcosm of UK society. Each day the King would set a construction task for the four private companies to undertake, in competition for money prizes. Players could choose to be workers, directors, managers, unemployed, media reporters, police, entrepreneurs, or parliamentary candidates. Participants were to sign up in one of these roles for the duration of the game. They were to subscribe ten pounds each to the treasury, which would remunerate players as decided by boards of government ministers and company directors. Companies and individuals could earn by entrepreneurship and royal patronage, or by criminal activity. The winners would be the individuals who had accumulated most money at the end of the game.

The first task set by the King was to design and construct a model town made from matchsticks. The best model at the end of a day would win a prize. On hearing this, entrepreneurs rushed into Cambridge town and bought up available supplies of matches. Players who nominated for parliament were voted on and ten members were elected. Self was elected Prime Minister. His cabinet set a minimum wage rate and an unemployment benefit, to be paid each day by the treasury from the subscribed funds.

In the meantime, managers and workers joined into companies. They milled around discussing where to obtain matches, architecture and how to construct a model. Work gangs used assembly lines to construct matchstick modules for other worker gangs to install. Enthroned in the Great Hall, the King conferred with parliamentarians and media.

Construction workers erected town precincts from pre-constructed modules. Model towns occupied the four corners of the Great Hall. Company architects had created palatial buildings with matchsticks, with cloisters lined by model trees and figurines strolling in ornamental gardens. They built elaborate features such as town halls and football stadiums.

Public media broadcasts spread rumours about designs, matches and theft. The companies employed guards to protect their construction sites from vandals and thieves. Self ordered the police to prevent lawlessness, but they said it was dangerous work and wanted a pay rise. When they didn't stop the thieves, they demanded further pay rises.

When town buildings included materials other than matches, there were protests that this gave an unfair advantage. The King made arbitrary rulings that he declared were just, but favouritism was suspected.

The King was abducted. Self as Prime Minister would not pay his ransom demanded. Media sources claimed Self's government was corrupt. He was dumped from the cabinet and suffered the indignity of collecting unemployment benefit. A new prime minister was elected on promise of a pay rise for everyone.

After working all day, construction was stopped and a panel of judges proceeded from model to model. Deciding a winner was controversial, because achievement criteria had not been announced and the King was still missing. Protests were noisy. Cash prizes were awarded and corporate treasurers paid their suppliers and workers. That ended the first day's play.

On the second and third days, the King had been found and he set further tasks for the companies to perform.

On the fourth day, the King addressed the assembled players.

'We have come to the end of the game,' he said. 'Your organisations have been dynamic. Police are the winners, because they have made most money. They were paid by the government, by the companies and by the criminals. The entrepreneurs who had monopolised the supply of matches are runners up, ahead of criminals who sold their stolen loot back to the companies. The media have been a liability to the community, publishing fake news and sensationalizing events, without helping to find the thieves, or to recover the King.

'You can draw your own conclusions about the attractiveness of living in this Society. My conclusion is that capitalist competition was inefficient but obtained some good results. Crime and police greed were at the forefront of problems.'

It was a conclusion worthy of the King's position at the Business School and exalted capitalism.

Self's brief time as Prime Minister warned him to avoid predation by corrupted media. He was forewarned of difficulties he could expect with any centrally planned resolution of the Cold War. He foresaw resistance and lost interest in both central planning and neo-liberalism. He continued his earlier interest in devolved planning. Devolution had been adopted by the companies for construction of the model towns. It was not a strategy they had chosen: the workers had copied devolution from other companies, because it offered pleasant working conditions and control over pay.

When he went back to London, Self looked in the real world for experience of devolved planning and found plenty. The Society Game had affirmed that devolution was feasible for the capitalist economies of the West and could be imitated by the Soviets. If adopted, it could end the Cold War.

CHAPTER 33
TEESSIDE

Self's research had found many possible models of UK national economic planning. His research supervisor sent him to get planning experience with an economics professor at York University. Teesside city council had many projects competing for social services funds and they had hired the professor to advise how to allocate the money fairly. Under his instruction Self devised and trialled, an algorithm for devolved government planning. Self hoped he could apply this method to uniting the Cold War belligerents.

Self was stationed in Teesside for three months. His task concerned allocation of funds to elderly, disabled, mentally ill and others in care with various conditions, including pregnancy. His task was to estimate benefits and costs for client types in order to calculate those provisions with the greatest return on investment.

Client relative costs were not available. They were devolved by default to the lowest level of the local government authority competent to decide budget outcomes, which was the political level. Costs were ranked from councillors' estimates.

When there was a change of government in Westminster, the Teesside Development Corporation's funds were seized centrally and the council's plans were left high and dry.

'I don't like your chances for getting money for devolved planning of social services,' said Nick. 'The Tories don't like social services; or planning; or devolution.'

'The new government is into centralisation either. Theirs is the complete opposite of my strategy,' Self complained.

The government had rejected Self's project, after two years, without proposing an alternative.

'You're on your own,' his supervisor told him.

Burke didn't have a PhD himself and he didn't seem to know what Self had to do to get one. Self found out external examiners should have been appointed. His thesis had to respect the examiners' disciplines and ontologies. Burke had not suggested anyone, leaving Self out on a limb.

Self had hoped his research experience would provide a technique he could adapt to unite the belligerents in the Cold War. But he had merely found out his research sponsors were not interested in devolution.

It was a disaster and he could hardly believe what had happened to him. In movies peoples' lives were sometimes upended by accidents, but this was no accident. His project had been binned without apology, after three years of his hard work, he had done on trust, nor had any alternative been offered.

It was simply a change of government in which the new regime had discarded all obligation to the previous regime. He was no longer wanted for anything by the system. He wasn't being counted on as a resource. His trust had been misplaced.

Chapter 34
Collision

It took several months for Self to realise his research project was mired in government bureaucracy. With his research delayed, Gretchen escalated the vehemence of her campaign to have a baby. But he expected to nail his thesis any day and then it would be only 12 months to write up and submit. After that they could have a baby.

'Will you be finished soon?' she asked.

'Please be patient,' Self told Gretchen. 'I'm doing something new and it will take time.'

Thesis submission processes were uncertain and his timing was not in his hands.

'You said you would be finished in 12 months. How much longer will you be?'

'I don't know.'

Always she pushed. He couldn't remember exactly how long he had said, but he knew he wouldn't be finished for at least another year.

Self read and read, desperately trying to interpret the partial cost-benefit data, his head spinning with political science, political economy, economics, sociology, social psychology and other disciplines. He wasn't nearly finished and needed money to keep going.

Desperately, Self tried to bring his research to a conclusion, opposed by Gretchen.

'We need money,' she snarled. 'You have been wasting time on your stupid research. Quit your PhD and get a job.'

He waited, fearing the worst, provoked to extreme anxiety by Gretchen's campaign to have a baby.

Then he received notification from the research grants authority that his three years was almost up and his grant payments would cease shortly. Self's grant would expire. It could possibly be extended for another year if he applied.

'I told you this would happen,' Gretchen said. 'I can't wait any longer. You've had your chance and blown it.'

This was false. He understood that having a child was of utmost importance to her, but the window of opportunity was closing because of her own deception. She had lied to him about her age and was already classified as elderly. Her campaign to have a baby was unilaterally demanding and discussion with her was always disagreeable. Self realised that Gretchen was the dragon who fought the lion in Nietzsche's fable, preventing him occupying the domain he had been striving for.

'Women can control their own fertility,' she said fiercely. 'We are not sexual objects and will no longer be used by men. Your misogyny won't work on me.'

'My pursuit of freedom is objective and without misogyny,' he said. 'We have an agreement and you are dishonouring it.'

He was already stressed and having a baby could be the final straw.

He wanted to push back against her but he didn't know how. His mother had been pushy and his father a pushover. Self was up against an obstreperous woman and he lacked instinct, weapons and support to get what he wanted.

The dragon was an ardent women's liberationist. She was locked onto a zero-sum gender war with Self, contesting his rights. Her disrespect for him contravened the principles of a civil marriage, her interest in him seeming loveless and selfish: he was merely a means for her to have a child. The loving partnership he expected and wanted was a romantic illusion.

Self's family opposed his PhD work too. They thought he should quit and get a job. His research work was without external validation, driven by his will alone.

A few weeks later the dragon made an announcement.

'I'm pregnant,' she told him.

It was the final treacherous straw in her campaign to block his academic career. It had been a condition of her moving in, that she had to wait until he finished his PhD to have a baby. She had dishonoured their agreement, knowing it would have serious repercussions for him. He inferred that not only did she not want him to succeed, she wanted him to fail. She had responsibility for contraception and she had betrayed him.

He would not let this setback affect his offspring.

'It will be different from now on,' he said.

Whereas his disagreement with Gretchen had concerned their mutual obligations to a theoretical offspring, the issue had now become Self's obligation to a real foetus and he was totally loyal. He had lost in his standoff with Gretchen and his dissent would not cast a shadow over the conception, or subtract from his care for the child. His instinct was to celebrate, minimising repercussions Gretchen had created.

Although they would have no income when she finished work, she immediately bought a ground floor semi-detached house in joint ownership without his approval, obtaining a mortgage with the last of her income and hypothetical employment she planned for him. She didn't seek his agreement and he was mortified to have to move his living place. She compounded his distress by exposing him to financial obligation and a change from a comfortable home to a house he disliked, in a suburb he disliked.

Sadly he made a heap of his notes and file cards in the garden and burned them. For three years he had laboured over them and now there was nothing left.

'Would you like a cup of tea,' he said proffering an olive branch to Gretchen.

She shook her head. Her antagonism was a fixture.

Sensing their discord, friends stayed away. Invitations to dinner dried up. Self was socially isolated and demoralised.

'Her treachery and opposition are disloyal,' Self thought. *'But there is nothing I can do about it, except leave her.'*

He lacked courage to desert his unborn child, even though Gretchen had been seized by the acrimonious spirit of the dragon that Nietzsche had identified as every lion's mortal enemy.

As he waited to hear if his grant extension had been renewed, he was tortured by apprehension. If he didn't get the money, he would have to abandon his PhD. He panicked at quitting with nothing, after three years of hard work.

Self was socially isolated and demoralised. Burke, his research supervisor, was a journalist who could write front page news stories, but was unfamiliar with PhD supervision processes and he had no interest in Self's chosen field. He failed to provide support essential for a grant extension, pulling the rug out from under Self. The extension was rejected without any correspondence with Self. He inferred that his thesis was opposed by both his supervisor and by the grants authority, the latter possibly for political reasons, such as Government antipathy to devolution. As for Burke's betrayal, it could only be incompetence.

Desperately Self tried to find something in his work that he could salvage and bring to fruition for a Master of Philosophy degree.

'Could you bring the two sides together somehow?' asked Nick.

'I have written to the religious leaders on both sides.'

He had been proud to promote interaction between the sides at the border.

'It will take more time than I have.'

But his colleagues disdained interaction at the border between the opponents, as vulgar politics. They regarded a conciliation posture as treachery. They couldn't see how religion could come into it.

'Their idea of ending the Cold War is to drop a big f**king bomb on the other side,' Self said.

It was the end of his devolution thesis. He had lost his domain.

'I'm so sorry, mate,' said Nick. 'They've let you down badly. You seem to have fallen through the cracks. What are you going to do?'

'There's not much I can do. I'll have to quit and get a job.'

Gretchen, was unsympathetic.

'You wanted to be a hero who ended the Cold War didn't you! You were a glory hunter, trying to be famous.'

'It's true I am ambitious to serve the public good, but how else would you want it?'

'I want you to quit. You are wasting your time.'

Gretchen undermined him. He lacked finance to bring his PhD work to fruition and he became sleepless worrying about it and mentally ill. He attended a day-care clinic for three months. His family lacked understanding and avoided him. His research was halted as he recuperated.

He readied their new home for a baby and started looking for a job. Part-time work was unavailable and he could not postpone his PhD work until later. He looked for professional engineering work, using skills he had acquired at Continental.

A friend employed him in his former profession, as a petroleum engineer, at his London office. It was work he was familiar with and he was a consultant with his own domain. He innovated statistical methods for exploring the North Sea. His technique was taken up by other engineers advising corporations and governments.

When their baby girl arrived, she was lovely but demanding, disrupting their lives. Things hadn't gone the way he wanted but he had a lovely child and responsibilities he would see through.

As if Self hadn't suffered enough already from the dragon, Gretchen struck again, announcing her return to Australia, whining that she didn't like London weather, reneging on their agreement to live in England. It would bring his new career to a halt.

'I am taking the baby,' she announced.

'I don't want to go to Australia yet,' he said. 'In a year or two.'

She ignored his NO to uprooting and going to her home country. It was the first time the possibility of going to Australia had been raised between them, but now she had made it an ultimatum. He was having success in his new career and he was earning enough in England for both of them to live comfortably until their baby could go to day-care.

Her plan could take his child away from him.

'You don't have to come,' she said. 'I'll get custody.'

Her readiness to separate him from their child was misandry and selfish. The baby had brought a new purpose to his life. The irony was that although she had interrupted his work, he loved the baby very much.

Going to Australia would sabotage his promising new career in the UK and he would have to start again in a new country, without any family support. Sadly he had to accept that he could never resume his PhD work. He would miss the UK and his family.

Self was no longer surprised by Gretchen's hostility. It was in her nature to oppose him and for the moment there was nothing he could do to stop her.

Outmanoeuvred by the dragon, he emigrated to Australia with Gretchen and the baby. As their liner edged out into the Solent, he held the baby and resolved to put behind him his awful PhD experience and make a new start in a new country.

CHAPTER 35
DIMORPHIC CONFLICT

In Australia, Self started a new career with Wattle Mines in Brisbane. He would supervise a contractor's scrapers and dozers excavating an open cut mine on the Darling Downs.

'It's an easy job,' the manager said. 'Take a book with you.'

Self had graduated as a chemical engineer in the UK, with no experience of supervising mining, nor of Australian miners. He was filling in for a mining engineer who had left the company to go to another job. He was responsible for safety and could be blamed if anything went wrong.

When he arrived at the mine, the scraper drivers were speeding crazily, likely to roll their machines. Self told them to slow down. They ignored him. The loaded scrapers had a low centre of gravity, which allowed them to slide into corners at high speeds. Self estimated that a scraper's slide on muddy ground could stop suddenly, causing it to overbalance and roll, injuring or killing the driver.

He tried persuading them and talked with the contractor's supervisor, but they continued to corner too fast, seeming to deliberately antagonise him. He was responsible for their safety and his opinion should be respected. Sensing his dismay, they drove even faster and he expected an accident at any moment. He learned later that they were 'rubbishing' him, an Australian sport of taking down of immigrants for fun.

He had other worries, at home. Gretchen was mid-term with their second baby. He realised she was intractably opposed to his becoming a lion in spirit, expressing contempt for his dominion as an engineer.

'Engineering is about things,' she said. 'Engineers don't know about people and get high salaries to bolster their over-large egos.'

Friction between Gretchen and Self continued. Her hostility was based on feminist misandry that prevented a balanced relationship. In the Proterozoic Era 2500 to 539 million years ago, the first animals on Earth split into female and male dimorphic forms to share responsibility for reproduction. Pairs collaborated for intercourse and protecting the young. The interdependence of the genders could have scaled up in descendent human pairings today. It was in their mutual interest to stay together and cooperate in raising young, but between Self and Gretchen there was harmful tension.

There had been a case of German measles at Gretchen's work and she was worried that she had been infected and the baby would be deformed. She was hyper-sensitive because she had worked with disabled children and with measles victims. When Self left her in Brisbane, to go to the mine, she worried incessantly. She hadn't had a test to resolve measles infection, nor a vaccination. She foisted her worries on to Self by phone, but there was nothing he could do. She had lost self-control, was panicking and when he went away to the mine, she fled to her parents' house.

Self's education had not prepared him to rationalise the prospect of a disabled child and with the added worry of the speeding drivers he couldn't sleep. With better interpersonal skills he might have defused the situation, but his anxiety stopped him from taking responsibility for the crazy drivers. After three sleepless nights in the mining town, he realised he was out of his depth and informed his boss in Brisbane.

'There is going to be an accident and I can't take responsibility,' he told him.

His boss flew there in a light plane and took Self home for a break.

He had wanted to be a lion but Gretchen's dysfunctional dimorphism halted their partnership. Gretchen had experience and advice on pregnancy worries, whereas Self had none and became overwrought. When he returned to Brisbane shell-shocked, she sent him away, alone and at risk. She continued to agitate and antagonise after the baby was born.

Their fears for the baby were groundless. The child was perfect. Self had once loved Gretchen, but her hostility and the stress of her demands when moving into their new home depressed him and affected his career. In those days there was no paternity leave. He had several weeks off work, seeming shamed by failing to do a job he was not trained for. His credibility for supervising mining had been accidentally destroyed and he was assigned to office work.

Self's career at Wattle Mines was stigmatised. His lion spirit was compromised. He had to revert to camel work but his experience in the desert had hardened him, like a cactus, beyond earthly suffering.

The second phase of feminism was in full flood and every aspect of Self's conduct was criticised by Gretchen, a dragon wife impelled by feminism and misandry. Women at that time were asserting, with success, rights to employment and careers equal to men's. Over the next three years, she minimised his role in raising the babies, undermining him, challenging his equal authority in deciding childcare. Against his wishes, she stopped breast feeding, placed their two toddlers in day-care and resumed full-time work.

'They are too little to risk day care by a stranger,' Self protested.

'You don't have any say in it,' she screamed. 'It's my call. I'm not going to stay home and look after them. I want a life. You stay home and look after them yourself.'

'Will you be able to match the pay I would lose?' Self said. 'I won't be able to continue in my job.'

'I can get only a half now, but it will increase.'

'We have a mortgage. Our lifestyle will take a hit. We would have to move to a smaller place closer to the city. Do you really want to put having a job ahead of providing a stable home and caring for the kids?'

Gretchen gave her work partial priority, obtaining a job with school hours, taking the children with her to and from day-care. When they were older and in primary school, she retrained and advanced her own career, taking a job with longer hours.

'This isn't working,' he told her. 'The children are being neglected. We have to arrange it differently.'

'It's not ideal but it's working.'

'I don't think it is,' he said. 'You have left me out of making arrangements for the kids. They are too little for day-care but you have pushed ahead like a bulldozer and done what suits you.'

'I'm not going to stay home and look after them,' she shrieked. 'I want to work.'

A few years later at high school they became 'latch-key kids', letting themselves into the house after school and playing unsupervised. Self was unhappy at this arrangement and apprehensive that the children were not safe, but he was locked into a high-salaried job. His hours were long, he travelled sometimes and when he arrived home the children had gone to bed.

Self sometimes had misgivings that he was being hard on Gretchen, that because she had given birth twice, childcare had naturally come her way, just as preparing family meals had started with breast feeding. Another extension was shopping for cooking ingredients. There was no logical reason why she had to do everything, but it had seemed convenient, for her, as well as for him. She took over his role.

Self wanted their small children to have a loving home and hoped that Gretchen had not divulged to them the unlikely circumstances of their births, as if his loyalty to them had been at fault, rather than hers. He hoped that Gretchen would not use their disputes to poison his children's relationship with him or undermine their security by revealing that he had wanted to delay their conception. He sensed her criticism in her uncompromising attitude towards him. Quarrels erupt between many couples and are forgiven, but Gretchen and he had deep-seated antipathy with ongoing differences.

Self was not convinced that her working was necessary.

'You have been the specialist home maker so far, but the children will benefit more when both of us are sharing the work,' he said. 'I'm looking forward to it. But it won't be easy for me to switch to being a part-time parent. The expectation at Wattle Mines has been that the company has first call on my time and working late sometimes or at a weekend is part of the job. I would have to take a back seat at lower pay, or look for another job.'

'The two of us couldn't work together,' she said.

'You need to try harder,' he said. 'It is part of human experience to share child raising. It begins with separate gender roles in reproduction and continues with male and female roles. Refusing to share them with me is harmful for the children and hurtful to me.'

'You aren't capable of sharing childcare.'

'I am perfectly capable,' he said. 'The problem is communication.'

'Rubbish,' she said. 'The messages have been getting through, but you have lacked empathy. You haven't understood or cared what I wanted.'

'I understand your self-seeking only too well,' Self said. 'Matters won't be improved by me getting another job and you working more. We wouldn't be able to share, even if we were castaways on an island. You are unable to flex. You want too much. You complain too much.'

'Me complain? Huh,' she scoffed. She always complained.

'We should support each other and help each other get what we want from life,' he said. 'The problem has been that you don't know how to share responsibilities without taking over. You have been prejudiced against me. You have a reflex for overriding my wants, deciding everything yourself. You have been a bully and your time is up.'

'Don't blame me because you can't cope.'

'I coped perfectly well until you barged into my life.'

Self's relationship with Gretchen had broken down and although they still lived together they seldom spoke.

Her hostility covered up her low confidence in him, already damaged when they first got together.

His employer wanted him to transfer interstate. He refused and they moved him away from his expertise into marketing. Relinquishing his lion domain, contested by Gretchen, was enormously liberating for Self, gaining involvement with his children at home. He reverted to slavery in the herd as a camel of limited reliability, away from his competence in engineering.

After eight years, Self quit Wattle Mines and became a school teacher, joining a herd with opportunities for camel work and school holidays with his own children.

It was a loveless marriage, within which they loved their children. Gretchen marginalised his involvement in raising the children, blocking him from caring tasks and continuity in understanding the children's progress and difficulties. Caught between their parents' animosity, their children learned to be independent.

CHAPTER 36
PATRICIDE

Living in Australia to be with his children, Self became estranged from his family in the UK.

Self visited them in the UK at intervals of about five years. He was hardly aware of his parents' aging and their inabilities came as a series of shocks. Caring for the elderly was seldom discussed in his parents' families. When his father's siblings couldn't care for themselves, they were cared for at home, first by family members and then eventually they were moved into a nursing home to wait to die. There would be family visits, but the situation embarrassed and depressed everyone and the old person seldom lasted more than a year or two in care.

An alternative was to employ a housekeeper, but a house without stairs would be needed. The cost of carers could become exorbitant and judged prohibitive by family, who were counting on inheriting that money. So the alternative was theoretical.

Because he lived in Australia, Self didn't hear much talk about provision for his parents' old age. He was the last to know when matters were decided. After he retired from teaching, an alternative of returning to live in the UK was an option for him, but by then arrangements for his parents had been made. Due to the resounding silence of his siblings, he preferred to live in Australia, his daughters' home country, where he had some community involvement through his writing.

When his father retired, he and Self's mother swapped homes with Self's older brother's family, who moved into the farm house. It was a move nearby and his father could keep in touch with farm activities. He found small jobs to do and kept himself busy for several years, but he developed partial dementia.

Self learned of his father's illness by letters to Australia from his mother and brother. He thought they were exaggerating his father's condition, because he spoke to him on the telephone fortnightly and there didn't seem to be much wrong. Self inferred that they had a summary care agenda, such as wanting to put his father in a home of some sort. He knew that finding a residential home for his father would be difficult, but there wasn't much he could do from Australia.

Self wrote to his father regularly, recalling times they had shared on the farm and his fond memories of people, places and events. He never knew of any response of his father to his two-weekly letters, or whether any of the family had helped him to read them.

It was evident that his mother was having difficulty looking after his father and wanted Self during his visits to relieve her daily burden of care for him. She felt responsible for her husband and wouldn't consider getting help. When Self visited, his mother sent him away with his father to visit his family in Yorkshire. These unplanned visits imposed on relatives and were an ordeal for Self. His father was compliant, but he was mostly either fuddled or silent in the passenger seat.

Self had refused to sign a document empowering his brothers as attorneys, to conduct his father's affairs, when he could no longer manage them. They had not told Self what their plans for his father were nor how they would exercise their authority. They seemed paralysed by an unfounded fear that Self would have his father write a new will. His will left his estate to the four siblings when their mother died. Self deduced they would seize his funds to put him in some type of residential care according to family tradition. Self knew that moving his father into a home, away from the farm and away from his wife, would be traumatic for him. He was able to delay matters by a year, extending his father's remaining freedom significantly.

'I am going to cut you out of my will,' his mother promised Self, when he would not sign the power of attorney.

The family did not reply to Self's letters and did not reassure him there were suitable plans for his father. They told him nothing about his father's affairs and when they moved him they withheld the new location. Self had to write to the solicitor who was his executor of his estate for his address. The solicitor managed for the trustees in a very high-handed manner, for ten years giving no progress reports on their investment of a fund the siblings would inherit. His two brothers were trustees but they seemed supremely self-interested, failing to honour their responsibility to Self.

He tried to start a conversation with them about caring for his father in old age, but they would not discuss it with him, nor had they done any planning that they mentioned. He could not draw his father into discussion of his living arrangements.

'Where would you like to live?' he asked his father.

He thought about it.

'Here?' he answered, with a shrug, as if it was theoretical.

None of the three UK siblings wanted to take care of his father, that was clear.

Self suggested his parents move into a bungalow with a housekeeper to clean and prepare meals. None of his siblings was interested. His parents' estates could afford it but his mother wouldn't accept meals on wheels as if she held a monopoly over domestic care. His siblings could have persuaded them to get help, but he supposed the cost would deduct from their inheritances. So they never applied for any state or private help when they needed it.

Next he heard his mother could no longer cope with his father because he had dementia. It seemed more likely she had chosen this moment to abruptly end her caregiving, precipitating severance, without offering a more humane solution for him.

When he returned to Australia, Self talked on the phone with his father fortnightly. His mother used to bring his father to the phone. When she refused to get him, he was surprised.

'He doesn't want to speak to you.'

Self didn't believe her. His father had always wanted to talk when he called. She seemed jealous because he had stopped talking with her, because she had become unpleasant. It was evident that his mother and father were at loggerheads.

'He's got dementia and he isn't worth talking to,' his brother said.

'He's a liability,' his sister said.

Self was outraged. He cared deeply for his father and missed talking with him. He had always found his father a capable conversant and now his mother was cutting him off from the man he dearly loved.

He wrote to family and friends asking them to arrange with his brother installation of a phone for him to speak to his father, to stop his mother blocking him. No phone was provided, he supposed, because his brother bullied people and the others didn't want to be involved in a dispute.

Self worried that they might harm his father and he arranged from Australia for a police officer to check he was well and being cared for. He was relieved when the policeman declared he was in a satisfactory condition.

The next time he went to the UK, his father was living in a home for residents with dementia. The place was chaotic, without privacy, without anywhere he could withdraw. When Self left, his father pleaded to 'go home', clawing at the door to get out.

His father was an honest and kind man, but they took away his comfort, social contact and dignity. Keeping him there was horribly cruel but there was no obvious alternative. He was active and mentally competent part of the time and seemed too well to go into a nursing home.

Self got his brothers attention by accusing them of trying to kill his father. It was overly dramatic, but six months later his father almost died in hospital. When he recovered, they moved him to a nursing home.

'I'd put him in that dementia home again,' said his brother. 'He doesn't know anything.'

Self had suggested they consider a nursing home.

When Self visited him again, his father was in a nursing home, grossly obese. He had a knee condition and couldn't support his own weight. The nurses used a crane to hoist him over the toilet.

His diet could have been contrived to induce massive weight gain and Self suspected family doing condoned by the nurses. He was shocked. Gretchen was with him and she had more experience but there was nothing he could do. Their visits with him comprised pushing his wheelchair into the garden. There was no conversation. His father had lost his dignity and died soon afterwards, seemingly by starving himself to death.

Self was devastated and grieved for years.

Attendance at his father's funeral would honour him and his siblings who had cared for him. He had done what he could to honour his parents by going to England when they were alive. His letters to his siblings were unanswered and it would have been hypocritical to attend to honour them.

Self made one further attempt to talk with his mother after his father's funeral. He went to England to talk with her but she was unreasonable and disagreeable. There was no discussion. She lived on in a nursing home for several years but he had no further contact with her, despite writing sometimes.

He sent letters to her at two weekly intervals, with many fondest memories. Self never knew whether anyone had read them to her, due to failing sight, or if she even received them.

Both funerals were in term time, when his students would be disadvantaged by his absence. Self wouldn't cross the globe to be with relatives who treated him with contempt.

His attendance, it seemed to him, would be an extravagance. It would not be appreciated by anyone, as far as he knew. There was no tradition calling him. His rejection by his family had begun when he left the farm to go to university, again when he became mentally ill and finally when he emigrated to Australia. He had no religious precepts requiring his attendance and if there was a God, he would see his parents again, hopefully free of family ties. He was a son who had not been tied by family relations and he was a brother whose love for his siblings had been rejected many times. So he watched both funerals on the internet.

The trustees of his father's estate distributed it to his children. The siblings were supposed to receive equal amounts but Self had no evidence that had been followed, despite requesting confirmation from his siblings. His brothers were trustees and had performed the office opaquely with ill grace. He received an amount most of which he passed to his daughters and they were grateful.

PART 6
CHILD

When Self quit engineering to teach school science and write textbooks, his marital conflict with Gretchen eased. During school holidays he saw more of his own children. He began writing fiction novels, becoming involved in writing groups, publishing and marketing his books on Amazon. When he retired from teaching, he wrote full-time. He wrote political thrillers, speculative science fiction, crime and philosophical novels.

It was a new multi-layered world, in which he could self-express. Theoretically there could be contradiction of his ideas, but he was protected by disclaimers that his characters, places and situations were fictional. It was his ideal life, doing what he liked, involved with open-minded people.

'The child spirit is innocent and forgetful, making a new beginning, taking risks to find what it wants from life, playing the game of creation, a self-propelling wheel, a first motion, a sacred Yes, its spirit affirming life and winning its own world.'
Nietzsche, Thus Spake Zarathustra, p22.

Self loved his life of parenting, teaching and writing. There was so much beauty and interest in the World. He advocated change for its own sake, often questioning values established by other people in past times. Many people's eyes looked down at the screens of their devices, seduced to acquire useless knowledge, paying for hollow online experiences and wasting their lives. Self concentrated on novel ideas, to be explored in thought and discussion, having alternatives for making the world a better place.

CHAPTER 37
BACK AT SCHOOL

Self had resigned from Wattle Mines because he was disaffected with the anti-intellectual ethos of the engineering there. Designs were imitative, adopting technologies off-the-shelf, without first checking them. He wanted his engineering work to have a more empirical approach. When he was transferred to marketing, he quit and retrained for a year to become a high school science teacher.

His objection to marketing was that it dealt in falsity. When a customer wanted to know characteristics of a product, Self's role was to find out the minimum specification acceptable and lie that his company's product would meet it. The work was dishonest and he quit. Teaching science was relatively honest and sincere.

It was an abrupt change of occupation. As a teacher, his work was more demanding and stressful, for half the pay. School students preferred their teachers to be younger and more flexible than his 40 years would allow. Younger teachers had ready responses to student provocation, whereas Self had to think what to do. His responses were cognitive, slower, sometimes mistaking small incidents that became problems. Teaching up to seven classes every day was gruelling and by the weekend his brain was mush.

To begin with, he thought he might be in a lion role at the school, but autocratic roaring was counter-productive. He made a role for himself as a facilitator of class learning, in which he tried to serve the students with the information and resources they wanted.

Teaching engaged him fully and in the evenings and weekends he tried to respond to the situation developing in the UK with his aging parents. The communication was intemperate, with little goodwill. The family squabble compounded without sensible voices, nor recognition of personal rights. It was a Camusian absurd world, void of meaning, in which chaos reigned.

Self clung to his teaching work in Australia, getting enormous satisfaction. Teaching enabled him to assume a childlike role in which his work, which had always demanded more attention than he had time for, now suddenly became intriguing, a delight and he could investigate subjects until he was satisfied. It was child's play and he could be as curious and as frivolous as he wanted.

His favourite science lessons were experiments, requiring prior preparation of materials, demonstration of techniques and discussion of results. A problem was that the school's laboratory assistants couldn't keep up with his demands for materials and equipment. Other science teachers' classes did little practical work. The other teachers complained Self was greedy, taking an unfair share of laboratories, equipment and science assistants.

Without lab gear, his default lessons were expository, imparting little understanding, or he would set station workshops, such as inquiries investigating displays he had assembled of samples, illustrations and artefacts. Without a home room, having to move everything around the school to his classes, setting it up each time, was demanding.

His science classes were seldom theoretical, usually demonstrating equipment and materials. He avoided equations and tried to get students working on practical assignments, such as teaching a new behaviour to a pet animal at home. His teaching was most successful with students who had been assessed as low achievers, limited by lack of success resulting from low interest, rather than from low ability. He motivated those that lacked success to work hard. In his lessons, they rediscovered self-worth and the joys of investigation and study.

He demonstrated phenomena from physics, chemistry, biology and earth science. He organised an all-night camp out under the stars, inviting a local astronomy association to bring their telescopes for students to look through. Students talked about celestial objects and space travel, realising how tiny were human concerns, within the immensity of the universe.

In Self's classes, students worked at their own pace, requesting teacher assistance when they needed it. His use of student self-direction was opposed by other teachers, committed to teacher-centric methods. Self's engagement with his classes took a toll on him physically and diverted his time from his own children and wife. They knew something was wrong, by comparing with neighbours.

'You and mum don't have affection,' his daughter Sarah observed. 'Next door, they enjoy being together. Their marriage has love.'

'Your mother and I love you,' was his reply.

When Sarah started university, she moved out from home. After that, they didn't see her for weeks at a time. When she graduated she started a postgraduate degree interstate and seldom came home. Wanting to distance herself from the tension at home could have kept her away.

Michael was still at school and he had a girlfriend when he was in senior. The two were inseparable and Self worried that Michael was too young to be tying himself down, but Gretchen did not share his concern. Self and Gretchen seldom agreed and Self thought that their children had an advantage of parental conflict, better than a façade of parental unity. Michael too moved out of home for university, possibly also to escape the rift between his parents.

Self quit his job at the high school, burned-out from stress of teaching lessons without enough practical science and unfair allocation of classes and rooms. When he refused to go back, he was reassigned to distance education, where teaching was online. The medium suited him better than face-to-face classroom teaching. His job became writing textbooks, with practical science to be done at home. It was a new world, in which he could self-express, develop and publish his fondest ideas. In distance education, with individualised programmes, students could make progress at their own rates.

When their children had left home, he and Gretchen missed them. She wanted to move and they uprooted from their home of the past 22 years. Self now lived close to his work and had more time for preparation. But living without their children was uneventful and their marriage slowly died. He was absorbed in writing textbooks and Gretchen received less and less attention. After several years of embittered interaction, she abruptly left him. When they divorced, he was relieved and grew into an overman, able to control his life. He forgot the entirety of their former marriage, because there were too many unhappy memories. He engaged enthusiastically in writing teaching materials and trialling experiments for his courses.

When he retired he began full-time writing of fiction novels in various genres. To him fiction was child's play. There was nothing diminutive about him, either physically or egotistically but he affected the spirit and naïveté of a child. Quitting teaching unburdened Self's spirit from countenancing rules, customs and conventions of society, that had in the past brought him into conflict with Gretchen and school administrators. His spirit became young again. He willed his own destiny, made up his own values, discovering for himself the meanings of things, without imposing on anybody else and existing in a liberated state of free creativity and play, like a child.

CHAPTER 38
FREEDOM WRITING

Self-the-child wrote novels. The time he spent writing formed the backbone of many of his days. His stories were memoirs with narratives woven as philosophies explaining his experiences. Some readers found that his writing quite abstruse. He had a predilection for relating events to theories, rather than presenting facts in isolation. He was sceptical of the fake science he found hiding within post-modern subjectivity, causal indifference, inference and ambiguity.

He was not discouraged when only a few copies of his books were sold. He was committed to writing as an activity, rather than having marketing goals. Most readers of fiction were women and although he targeted smart, intelligent and curious women, his books were based on his experiences and had mainly male characters. His child spirit, curious and playful, became immersed in the spirit world, exploring for persons, events, places and things to write about. He blogged ideas and had a small following who encouraged him. It kept him pleasantly occupied.

Without the dragon now, Self was unburdened of the rules, customs, history and conventions with which Gretchen had opposed him. He could make up his own values and apply them in novel situations. It was a new beginning, a game of taking wanted risks. His writing was composed and coloured with the freedom of an artist. He was an artiste.

Self deliberated and elaborated reflections from his experiences that stimulated his thinking. Viewed head on, reflections merely arranged images in order of proximity to the subject, like a mirror, reversing handedness. An oblique viewpoint had less familiar images, providing a side view of the subject that could be entertaining. When the angle of incidence of his gaze was acute, the reflected image angle was equally acute, revealing a distorted perspective, a novel view, which he could express in prose.

Many people prefer thinking about something new rather than reconsidering old experiences. Revisiting the past sometimes discovered contradictory events and embarrassing perspectives.

When people avoid distinguishing themselves and are disappointed when they don't attract others' interest, it can be a paradox. Perhaps, unintentionally, they are unfashionable, or choked by performance anxiety, or simply unaware of how self-contradictory they appear to others. Self's teaching had to be self-aware and stay relevant to students' interests, or he would be unable to lead their learning.

Readers of a memoir expect to read about exceptional experiences the author has had. Self wrote about 'scrapes' in which the spirit of a flawed character transcended, like Zarathustra's, rather than adulating a monolithic and successful character. The memoir illustrates universal spirit characters presaged by Nietzsche.

In Nietzsche's book, Zarathustra was a writer who planned how he would use his time. Zarathustra was . . .

'. . . *devoted to writing only his best and worthiest hours.*'

Self was most creative when his brain was rested, imagining the earliest ideas he stored could be the first to be accessed, by the FIFO principle, first in first out. Others used it to manage perishable goods, turning over stock items, giving them time to mature, before they would lose currency, as news items did. He watched himself choosing topics and words, aware of his physical condition and alertness, wanting to capture true experiences in words that would be remembered.

He usually rose early and after eating fruit, took a cup of coffee into his study and sat at his computer. He worked through the cool hours of the morning, getting up to look out from his balcony at the joggers and walkers passing in the park. In the afternoon he would siesta, then write again in the evening. It was a routine with new thoughts set in familiar places. Time slipped by easily.

He emulated the measured lifestyle of a great philosopher, Immanuel Kant (1724–1804) in Konigsberg, who was exceedingly regular in going for a daily walk and dining with guests. He divided time at the table into three equal parts. First, guests in turn related their activities to each other. Next the company analysed the anecdotes. The final third was given over to hilarity. It was a structure within which his fame as an original thinker blossomed.

Friedrich Nietzsche (1844-1900) was a prodigy, with his writing read by infamous leaders, including Hitler and Stalin, but he became ill with syphilis and madness. He was a great thinker and writer opposed to religion and monarchism. Zarathustra was his most successful book during his lifetime, but after his death and revision by his sister, his other writing became popular too.

Nietzsche's spiritual character Zarathustra metamorphoses into certain animal characters, camel's and lions, having traits with propinquity to familiar human aspirations. Although constancy of character is a virtue in literature, metamorphosis of character may be more usual than is commonly admitted. The *volte-face* of changing from camel-subservience to lion-domination can be found in some human lives, but it is not always understood as spiritual maturation. Without the Zarathustra template, Self's character could have been construed as flaky and unreliable.

Self wrote biographical memoirs in which the phases of his transcendent careers mirrored Nietzsche's allegory, eventually embracing Zarathustra's spirit of the child, unburdened by rules, free of conventions and heedless of historical precedents.

Niezsche's ideas and lifestyle have been criticised and Self's actions were sometimes controversial. He believed in free speech, but wanted the public to be educated not to take offense, except by legal action, observing laws of defamation, incitement, obscenity, fraud, confidentiality and others. He was daring and precocious. For those who could be offended easily, such as children, additional protection would be needed.

Self-in-retirement has been framed as Nietzsche's 'child' spirit, playful, curious and hopeful. This character culminated the series of three metamorphoses designated by Zarathustra, completing his spiritual transcendence.

PART 7
IMMORTAL

Self had been a camel, then a lion and finally a child.

The question which Self's story has tried to answer is: *What purposes compelled Self's spirit to transform and were they fulfilled?* Whereas each of the stages is remarkable, understanding of the whole series of changes needs explanation to relate them to each other and to the whole, with an ending, or was the final stage immortal?

CHAPTER 39
REINCARNATION

Self in the beginning is, like Zarathustra, seeking an individual role as a young camel, caste in a herd migrating through a desert. He differentiates himself by serving others, which would have Christian value, but Nietzsche denies existence of any God and has his spirit serve his own aspirations, realising his utility to others and regarding his role as a slave-like beast of burden, in a position of subjugation.

He grows an ego and seeks personal control of a domain, requiring a lion's courage and daring. When the lion is confronted by a dragon, he opposes it with tenacity and perseverance. He is at first curious about the world, but declines continual fighting with the dragon and relinquishes adult concerns, engaging in a playful existence, like a child who is unaware of morality, customs, traditions and systematic exploration of alternatives. The spirit is creative and lives his life in the moment, between past and future experiences.

Nietzsche held a profound belief in the possibilities of human beings and wrote guidelines for those who shared his disdain for traditional religion, values, taboos and sacred cows. He was disdainful of those herd animals who do not wish to carry, take risks, stick together and instead rely on the shepherd to show them what is good for them. In his view, they are slaves.

I have poured Self's careers in the real world into Nietzsche's moulds. Where they don't exactly fit the fable, Self's characteristics connect with the metamorphoses.

What drove Self's spirit to become a camel, then a lion, then a child? It took place over his working life. Did his ambitions change? Did the social settings of his work change? Did the meaning of his work slowly emerge? Or was his life a series of responses to evolving events?

The spirit lived in ways Zarathustra wanted us to follow. He preached 'life-affirmation', as honest and courageous questioning of all doctrines that hold people back. It is a toolkit enabling them to become '*ubermensch*', supermen, with mastery over their emotions and taking joy in simply existing and creating.

Nietzsche's fable does not present a 'food chain' to sustain the spirit. It took Self many years to find his place in the herd and distinguish himself as a camel. Nor does the camel fall prey to the lion, who worked hard to become a ubermensch, a superman and acquired the wherewithal to claim a domain, requiring him to slay a fierce dragon. The camel spirit aspires to be a lion spirit. Although in the story the lion and dragon become betrothed, they do not parent the child as a new incarnation. The child spirit emerges as an escape from the hostilities between the lion and dragon. The dragon spirit aspires to defeat the lion. The lion spirit yearns to be a child spirit.

Self progresses from an acolyte engineer, working in near-slavery, to a domineering lion who fights a dragonish wife for dominion over his family and territory. The narrative has Self forsaking his family, students and responsibilities, to bury himself like a child in playful study and writing.

Self's spirit is free at each stage to acquire characteristics needed to transform to the next stage, fulfilling that purpose. The spirits did not carry forward materials from the previous stage, or even accumulate wisdom. Of the spirits, the latest, the child, is least burdened by knowledge and history. The child spirit is wisest, yet is fulfilled through curiosity and experimenting, rather than by advising others.

This sequence may be fanciful, but it has a certain elegance that makes Self responsible for many errors, including his selfish intentions and reaction against the dragon. Before Nietzsche, one's actions and fate were caused by God, virtue and morality, beyond personal control. Nietzsche eliminated God and regarded what people did as either unconscious or under voluntary control. He wanted man to take control of his life with courage to seek greatness.

The courage Nietzsche wanted in his supermen was not held in mind briefly but in every cell of his being, like soldiers attacked by enemy fire, or like Pompeiians living beside a Vesuvian volcano that could erupt at any moment, or like residing in a flood-prone home by a river when it is raining heavily. For them, courage is not an attitude, it is behaviour that nothing can deter.

Self was strong-willed, like the camel spirit in Nietzsche's story. He regarded his engineering job as virtual slavery and strove for a territory of his own. His opportunity, to rule a domain like a lion, was contested by a hostile marriage partner, Gretchen. He became a superman and devoted himself to creation of novels.

Nietzsche saw the 'child' as a logical place to finish his story, as if the spirit could continue on and be reincarnated. Self reaches the end of his journey and because he is mortal, he cannot relive the memories by reincarnation and so the story will end when he dies. As if life can be circular, an old person can before dying gain new living with the simplicity and innocence of childhood. Self's spirit could repeat childhood and live earlier parts of his own story again, returning to earlier conditions.

Self learned from his father's demise to respect family and friends leading up to a dignified end. He wanted to stay healthy, avoiding illnesses, especially dementia which felled his father.

'To avoid dementia, you have to get out of your comfort zone,' he learned from Dr Michael Moseley, who compared three pastimes: Sudoku; jogging; and nude portraiture, for brain stimulation. Sudoku rated poorly, but nude portraiture was most beneficial, with jogging in between. Self sketched nudes for two years. Moseley's explanation was that the brain is most stimulated when it is out of its comfort zone. When sketching nudes became old hat, Self joined a choir at the university. He sang in the bass section of a choir of 60 voices, with an orchestra, performing Haydn's 'Harmoniemesse' Salve Regine in E, Mass #14 in B-flat Major. He had learned to read the score and sang many of the notes, some of them correctly.

'The choir was a mind-blowing experience,' he recalled. 'When we reached the Credo and the sopranos standing beside me turned their vocal power up to maximum volume, I was right out of my comfort zone. The hair stood up on the nape of my neck. It was thrilling. Then the soloists joined in ecstatic harmony in the Agnus Dei and afterwards blasted out the Donna Nobis. It would have set any dementia back years.'

It didn't come naturally to him to always seek the discomfiture needed but he figured that his sublime musical experiences would equally rout the lazy brain cells that were his enemy.

New musical experiences could be his salvation.

CHAPTER 40
Cold War

Without funding to compete his research, Self had to quit his PhD after three years. He kept in touch with other researchers monitoring Cold War developments. There were snippets of news about cross-border correspondence and interaction. Mutual respect between the two sides was growing and a new unity appeared that could undo the centrally-inspired hostile posturing of the superpowers. The solution he had proposed had not been sanctified by academia, but it seemed to be working. His idea to encourage opponents near the border to engage in joint religious worship was gaining interest. Although it was too late to resurrect his PhD, he now had practical experience and could relate happenings near the border to de-escalation of the conflict.

Clergy were already crossing the East-West border. The Berlin Wall was regarded as a barrier between families, friends and congregants, rather than dividing ideologically opposed peoples from preference or for their safety. Between religious congregations there was ideological connection across the border bringing the sides together. Strategies for 'mending bridges' between the belligerents developed and could have led to the opening of the Berlin Wall.

Thatcher and Reagan laid the foundations of neo-liberalism, with financial implications that undermined the nuclear arms race. In the UK, because interest was withdrawn from Self's proposal for devolution of planning and his research grant was not renewed, it was perceived he was a victim of politics rather than championing a lost cause.

Self reverted to engineering and then to teaching science.

Thirteen years after Self arrived in Australia, the Berlin Wall was destroyed and the Cold War ended. Self was overjoyed. It was the holy grail he had played a small part in finding. He felt vindicated. He had advocated devolution of central planning controls and they had enabled joint planning at the border. Perhaps the spiritual seeds he planted had grown into peace. Self didn't mind that his contribution went unrecognised. It was the peace he wanted.

The peacemaking philosophy was Nietzsche's will to power was, which exorcised religion, tradition, history and morality. They left cracks in the Wall, enabling it to be pulled down.

'I told you this would happen,' Self told Gretchen. 'I can't claim that I caused it but I foresaw how it could happen and proposed devolution, which is how it occurred. It took about six years for my plan to be adopted.'

'Huh! You are the only one who believes that.'

'When you hear a better explanation, let me know.'

'They said that local people crossed over.'

'An official announced people could cross on November 9th, 1989, exactly as I had planned.'

'You get no credit for hindsight,' said Gretchen bitterly.

'You really don't get it, do you, that an event can occur from many causes? I was one cause among many.'

'Yes, a lost cause,' she said nastily.

'You lost,' he said. 'Me.'

The ideological conflict between socialism and capitalism played a crucial role in shaping the events that led to the dissolution of the Soviet Union and the end of the Cold War era with the collapse of the Soviet Union in 1991. The victory of the capitalist, market-oriented system over the socialist model was a defining moment in the history of the Cold War. America and the Western allies had won.

Self's preoccupation with ending the Cold War had commenced when he was a young hippy and had lasted 20 years. He had instinctively focussed on the iconic tall trees of the conflict, socialism and capitalism, without being aware he was hacking his way through a wood. He had felled the tallest timber, letting in enough light for devolved capitalism to grow in the clearings. The adversity he had encountered had perhaps been typical for a non-aligned foot soldier, covertly fighting for peace. He was happy to be alive.

It had been a struggle but he felt vindicated. He would enjoy working on research for another story from within a different career and with a new goal, probably a writing goal. He regarded himself as fortunate in always having sustaining work. He imagined his childish spirit proposing a solution to another superpower impasse, bringing peace without bloodshed. There was hope for the World after all.

EPILOGUE

Self's careers had followed Nietzsche's allegory as if it was of universal significance. A spirit begins in a desert, joins a herd and tries to dominate, until opposed by a dragon, when it adopts a playful posture.

Self's responsibilities had increased, with industrial accidents, hippy stunts and partnership in a boutique. He learned to help his group at work with computing. He had eventually realised that engineering was a difficult career for his creative spirit to follow. He needed a doctorate to manage the herd. His attempt to carve out a domain doing university research was thwarted by a dragon spirit, who became his wife and opposed his spiritual development. She forced him to emigrate, where he joined a mining company, who used him badly. He became a school teacher and writer.

Experience of herd conditions was mandatory for camel work. His promotion to a management lion was delayed by his lack of empathy with subordinate herd members. Had he been more aware of this he could have pandered to the hierarchy, instead of being locked in combat with his dragon wife, Gretchen. It was a conflict he regretted and might have avoided if he had opposed the dragon more strongly as soon as she started constraining his life. He could have quit the fray earlier, following a more artistic career where his creativity could have been better recognised than was his attempted PhD. He found teaching rewarded him better and he became a writer of student textbooks. They were a springboard into fiction writing, which remained his ideal occupation, continued during his retirement.

Nietzsche's fable reveals a series of transformations of Self's spirit but his book focusses on his work relationships and his role as a superman. Self has setbacks but his spirit always moves onward and upward, through truth and justice towards a better tomorrow. It is a wider perspective within which Self's will-to-power and daring are exalted. Self encounters situations in which he lacks the power and resilience to effect change for the public good. Self is helped by his alter ego Superman, a wholly good hero with limitless power serving mankind.

He came of age as a capable young man who gave himself to action and excitement. He earned his place in the herd with his contemporaries, learning to serve the group. He yearned to have his own show but he was overly ambitious and held back by those whose help he needed. He changed to an occupation that suited him better and achieved the domain he had sought. Then he took up writing first as a hobby, then as a new career and finally to write an epilogue.

If there is any significance for the associations in this story, between Self's career events and Zarathustra's metamorphoses, it is that human endeavours are regulated by social and psychological conditions pertaining to migration of wild herd animals, attendant predators, nemeses and subliminal beings on a spiritual savannah. For sixteen years, Self was part of a migrating herd. His transcendence followed ancient rituals of professional workers, emerging eons before Friedrich Nietzsche wrote the story of Zarathustra. If the story had not mirrored human experiences, it would not be so preserved and treasured.

During a working life that was usually carefully controlled, Self had untidy and unhappy social episodes involved with his parents' family and with Gretchen. They took advantage of his social naïveté and exploited him. Too late, he learned to say NO and withdrew from them.

Although the contribution of his ideas for ending the Cold War did not achieve academic fame for him, it was congruent with historic events, vindicating his large effort. Without his solution, the Cold War confrontation could have resulted in global conflagration. His persistence with unpopular ideas held back his career, but it offered alternatives to the madness of the Cold War. His free spirit and stubborn independence were essential, from learning to ride a wild horse.

www.ingramcontent.com/pod-product-compliance
Lightning Source LLC
Chambersburg PA
CBHW051434290426
44109CB00016B/1553